Leonard G. Brown.
May. 1919.
—"—

Library of Historic Theology

EDITED BY THE REV. WM. C. PIERCY, M.A.

DEAN AND CHAPLAIN OF WHITELANDS COLLEGE.

CHRISTIANITY AND OTHER FAITHS

W. ST. CLAIR TISDALL, D.D.

LIBRARY OF HISTORIC THEOLOGY

EDITED BY THE REV. WM. C. PIERCY, M.A.

Each Volume, Demy 8vo, Cloth, Red Burnished Top, 5s. net.

NEW VOLUMES NOW READY.

MARRIAGE IN CHURCH AND STATE.
By the Rev. T. A. Lacey, M.A. (Warden of the London Diocesan Penitentiary).

THE BUILDING UP OF THE OLD TESTAMENT.
By the Rev. Canon R. B. Girdlestone, M.A.

CHRISTIANITY AND OTHER FAITHS. An Essay in Comparative Religion.
By the Rev. W. St. Clair Tisdall, D.D.

THE CHURCHES IN BRITAIN. *Vols. I. and II.*
By the Rev. Alfred Plummer, D.D. (formerly Master of University College, Durham).

CHARACTER AND RELIGION.
By the Rev. the Hon. Edward Lyttelton, M.A. (Head Master of Eton College).

MISSIONARY METHODS, ST. PAUL'S OR OURS?
By the Rev. Roland Allen, M.A.

THE RULE OF FAITH AND HOPE.
By the Rev. R. L. Ottley, D.D. (Canon of Christ Church, and Regius Professor of Pastoral Theology in the University of Oxford).

THE CREEDS: THEIR HISTORY, NATURE AND USE.
By the Rev. Harold Smith, M.A. (Lecturer at the London College of Divinity).

THE CHRISTOLOGY OF ST. PAUL (Hulsean Prize Essay).
By the Rev. S. Nowell Rostron, M.A. (Late Principal of St. John's Hall, Durham).

The following works are in Preparation :—

BIBLICAL ARCHAEOLOGY.
By Professor Edouard Naville, D.C.L.

THE PRESENT RELATIONS OF SCIENCE AND RELIGION.
By the Rev. Professor T. G. Bonney, D.Sc.

THE CHURCH AND THE INDIVIDUAL.
By the Rev. W. J. Sparrow Simpson, D.D.

POPULAR OBJECTIONS TO CHRISTIANITY.
By the Rev. C. L. Drawbridge, M.A.

MYSTICISM IN CHRISTIANITY.
By the Rev. W. K. Fleming, M.A., B.D.

RELIGIOUS EDUCATION: ITS PAST, PRESENT, AND FUTURE.
By the Rev. Prebendary B. Reynolds.

THE CHURCH OUTSIDE THE EMPIRE.
By the Rev. C. R. Davey Biggs, D.D.

THE NATURE OF FAITH AND THE CONDITIONS OF ITS PROSPERITY.
By the Rev. P. N. Waggett, M.A.

AUTHORITY AND FREETHOUGHT IN THE MIDDLE AGES.
By the Rev. F. W. Bussell, D.D.

THE ETHICS OF TEMPTATION.
By the Ven. E. E. Holmes, M.A.

EARLY CHRISTIAN LITERATURE.
By the Rev. Wm. C. Piercy, M.A.

GOD AND MAN, ONE CHRIST.
By the Rev. Charles E. Raven, M.A.

GREEK THOUGHT AND CHRISTIAN DOCTRINE.
By the Rev. J. K. Mozley, M.A.

THE BOOKS OF THE APOCRYPHA: THEIR CONTENTS, CHARACTER, AND TEACHING.
By the Rev. W. O. E. Oesterley, D.D.

THE GREAT SCHISM BETWEEN THE EAST AND WEST.
By the Rev. F. J. Foakes-Jackson, D.D.

Full particulars of this Library may be obtained from the Publisher.

LONDON: ROBERT SCOTT.

CHRISTIANITY AND OTHER FAITHS

AN ESSAY
IN COMPARATIVE RELIGION

BY THE REV.

W. St. CLAIR TISDALL, D.D.

LATE JAMES LONG LECTURER ON ORIENTAL RELIGIONS

AUTHOR OF "THE RELIGION OF THE CRESCENT," "THE NOBLE
EIGHTFOLD PATH," "THE ORIGINAL SOURCES OF THE
QUR'ÂN," "RELIGIO CRITICI," "COMPARATIVE
RELIGION," "MYTHIC CHRISTS AND
THE TRUE," ETC

LONDON: ROBERT SCOTT
ROXBURGHE HOUSE
PATERNOSTER ROW, E.C.
MCMXII

" If the Gospel is a revelation of the eternal
through facts of time, it cannot be treated simply
as one religion among others.   Given the revelation
of God, Comparative Religion may help to show us
how the forces of human nature clothed it with
religions of men ; but the application of Comparative Religion to the revelation itself is a funda-
mental error."

(GWATKIN : *Early Church Hist.*, vol. i., pp. 2, 3.)

———————

" Fecisti nos ad Te, et inquietum est cor nostrum
donec requiescat in Te."

(ST. AUGUSTINE.)

▼

EDITOR'S GENERAL PREFACE

IN no branch of human knowledge has there been a more lively increase of the spirit of research during the past few years than in the study of Theology.

Many points of doctrine have been passing afresh through the crucible; "re-statement" is a popular cry and, in some directions, a real requirement of the age; the additions to our actual materials, both as regards ancient manuscripts and archæological discoveries, have never before been so great as in recent years; linguistic knowledge has advanced with the fuller possibilities provided by the constant addition of more data for comparative study; cuneiform inscriptions have been deciphered, and forgotten peoples, records, and even tongues, revealed anew as the outcome of diligent, skilful and devoted study.

Scholars have specialized to so great an extent that many conclusions are less speculative than they were, while many more aids are thus available for arriving at a general judgment; and, in some directions at least, the time for drawing such general conclusions, and so making practical use of such specialized research, seems to have come, or to be close at hand.

Many people, therefore, including the large mass of the parochial clergy and students, desire to have in an accessible form a review of the results of this flood of new light on many topics that are of living and vital interest to the Faith; and, at the same time, "practical" questions—by which is really denoted merely the application of faith to life and to the needs of the day—have certainly lost none of their interest, but rather loom larger than ever if the Church is adequately to fulfil her Mission.

It thus seems an appropriate time for the issue of a new series of theological works, which shall aim at presenting *a general survey* of the present position of thought and knowledge in various branches of the wide field which is included in the study of divinity.

The Library of Historic Theology is designed to supply such a series, written by men of known reputation as thinkers and scholars, teachers and divines, who are, one and all, firm upholders of the Faith.

It will not deal merely with doctrinal subjects, though prominence will be given to these; but great importance will be attached also to history—the sure foundation of all progressive knowledge—and even the more strictly doctrinal subjects will be largely dealt with from this point of view, a point of view the value of which in regard to the "practical" subjects is too obvious to need emphasis.

It would be clearly outside the scope of this series to deal with individual books of the Bible or of later Christian writings, with the lives of individuals, or with merely minor (and often highly controversial) points of Church governance, except in so far as these come into the general review of the situation. This detailed study, invaluable as it is, is already abundant in many series of commentaries, texts, biographies, dictionaries and monographs, and would overload far too heavily such a series as the present.

The Editor desires it to be distinctly understood that the various contributors to the series have no responsibility whatsoever for the conclusions or particular views expressed in any volumes other than their own, and that he himself has not felt that it comes within the scope of an editor's work, in a series of this kind, to interfere with the personal views of the writers. He must, therefore, leave to them their full responsibility for their own conclusions.

Shades of opinion and differences of judgment must exist, if thought is not to be at a standstill—petrified into an unproductive fossil; but while neither the Editor nor all their readers can be expected to agree with every point of view in the details of the discussions in all these volumes, he is convinced that the great principles which lie behind every volume are such as must conduce to the strengthening of the Faith and to the glory of God.

That this may be so is the one desire of Editor and contributors alike.

W. C. P.

London.

Introduction

A CHRISTIAN undertakes the examination of non-Christian faiths with great sympathy and much interest. He is aware that all truth, wherever found, is of God. He knows that " we can do nothing against the truth, but for the truth," and that the truth will finally prevail. As himself a follower of Him Who is the Truth, he welcomes on the part of others all investigation which has really for its object the attainment of true knowledge. Christianity has nothing to fear but much to hope from the fullest enquiry. What is to be feared is carelessness, indifference, credulity. There is danger lest the ignorant and unstable should be led astray through very partial knowledge, and through blind reliance upon the assertions of men of strongly biassed imagination—such men as speak of the late Hindû fable of how Kṛishṇa went up to the sky to restore the goddess Aditi her earrings [1] as " parallel " to the Gospel account of our Lord's Ascension, and as probably the " source " of the latter. Others of the same bent of mind give long and very precise details regarding the most secret doctrines of the Mithraists, drawn from *non-existent* Mithraic scriptures. Upon this baseless fabric of a dream they found serious arguments. Others resemble the notorious Notovitch,

[1] Vide p. 159.

who boldly invented a Tibetan Gospel, "the Unknown Life of Christ." Of course, when enquiry was made, the monks at the monastery where the pseudo-Gospel had been "found" had never heard of it, and denied that it had ever existed.[1] The forger was so careless, so ignorant, or so confident of the credulity of the public, that he actually makes the supposed Brâhman author in the first century of our era, call our Lord by the name *Issa*, an evident corruption of the Arabic '*Îsa*', the existence of which name cannot be proved before the seventh century. Another Ananias tells the story[2] of "Jezeus Christna," which he says he learnt in South India ; being ignorant of the fact that no genuine Indian tongue contains the letter *z*, and trusting that it would never be discovered that not a single one of the statements which he declares he learnt from certain specified Sanskrit books occurs there at all.

But when, leaving all such unscrupulous writers and those who are merely ignorant and imaginative, we turn to the examination of the genuine tenets of non-Christian religions, ancient and modern alike, savage or civilized, we rightly expect to find much that is both interesting and instructive in them, whether these beliefs are enshrined in ancient writings or handed down by oral tradition. Human nature is very much the same everywhere, and so are human needs. It is useful and sometimes pathetic to learn what men, in ancient times for instance, thought and believed and hoped on the greatest of all subjects ; what solutions they proposed

[1] Vide Mr. J. A. Douglas' account in the *Nineteenth Century* for April, 1896.
[2] Vide p. 34, note.

to the deep problems of life and death, sin, suffering, and the object of existence. These Gentiles were in some cases our ancestors according to the flesh. Many of them were men of wisdom and intellectual power. All of them needed, and some of them earnestly sought for, spiritual light and guidance. For all of them the Son of God, in the fulness of time, lived and died and rose again. In some degree the True Light " lighteth every man coming into the world." What degree of that light, then, had reached these and other men of the past ? What knowledge of God and of the Way of Salvation is possessed by those who now live in unevangelized lands ? In what relation does Christianity stand to the faiths which preceded the proclamation of the Gospel ? These are a few of the many questions which naturally occur to the mind when an opportunity presents itself of becoming acquainted with some at least of the religions of the world.

Other questions arise as to the origin of Christianity itself as a religious system. How far is it a revelation from God, and how far has it borrowed from earlier religions ? In what do asserted resemblances consist, and to what are they due ? An earnest and reverent enquiry into such matters cannot fail to be of intellectual and spiritual benefit. One possible result may be that we shall ask ourselves seriously to what extent the surviving non-Christian faiths, such as Hindûism, and even religions of quite recent origin like Islâm, can possibly supply spiritual guidance and nourishment to men like ourselves; how far such religions would strengthen, comfort, enlighten *us*, if we were left to them, and whether we are justified in keeping to ourselves the light which all men need and to which all alike have a right.

In our investigations we shall be unable to deal fully with all these questions. Upon some of them, indeed, our limits will prevent us from touching at all at present. One object of this volume, however, will be attained if it leads men to think for themselves, and to study such questions independently, with a solemn sense of responsibility.

We shall not endeavour to exclude from consideration all matters of philosophy. The reason of this is obvious. We find a great deal of philosophy in all religions, even in those of savages. As Dr. Tylor truly says, "The religion of rude tribes is at the same time their philosophy." It is possible that much of mythology, which now seems unmeaning, is due to a misunderstanding of philosophical speculations. The cosmic egg, which occurs in so many religions, in Finland as well as India, in Egypt and in the New World, is an example of this. It shows that something in the nature of a theory of evolution existed long before the time of Democritus and Epicurus. Hardly clearer evidence of the existence of philosophy is afforded by the *Rig-Veda* hymn which enquires, "Who knows whence this product (*Prakṛiti*, Nature) originated ? " [1] Religion, on the other hand, enters very largely into the philosophy of Plato and most other philosophers. In this book we shall not go deeply into any philosophical system, for our concern is primarily with religions only. But when philosophic ideas have, in certain cases, become thoroughly incorporated into a religion (as Pantheism has into Hindûism), or have largely taken its place, as in China, it is necessary to consider them as constituting an integral part of the religion as it actually exists. Thus the doctrine of fate is inseparable from Islâm,

[1] Vide p. 56.

Hindûism, and the religions of ancient Greece and Rome. Yet belief in it is doubtless due to philosophy. Are Nemesis and the Furies less the creatures of philosophy than are the doctrines of Karma and Transmigration?

In our day an attempt has been made to substitute for Christianity a kind of eclectic system of ethics by culling carefully chosen moral sentiments from the books of many religions. This is very interesting when the passages thus selected mean what they are taken to mean, though oftentimes they are entirely misunderstood. But, after all, the attempt to form anything like a religion in this way is hopeless. It is like collecting specimens for a museum. No amount of care in selecting can give either of such collections vitality. Life is lacking, and religion is nothing without life. In making his collection the collector is, of course, dominated by his own preconceived idea of what he wishes to gather together. In religious and ethical anthology-making, the plan is influenced, directly or indirectly, by Christianity, even when the collector aims at finding something better, in his opinion, than the corresponding Christian doctrine or precept. But no one has succeeded in our time in forming a religion in this way, any more than, were he to collect every bone of the skeleton of a megatherium, he could make the creature live. That such a way of constructing a religion now is doomed to fail is a sufficient answer to the theory that Christianity is an eclectic system formed in precisely this manner. In Christianity every truth fits into its own place as a living part of a living organism, and the harmonious working of the whole shows the wisdom with which it has been designed, while its vitality has been drawn from no merely human source, for " Christ is our Life."

As a final warning against being misled in such studies as those to which this book is devoted, and as an illustration of the way in which even men of learning often permit themselves to be led astray by their own fancy, it may not be out of place to quote here a passage from a recent book, the object of which is to show that Christianity and Mahâyâna [1] Buddhism are very much the same thing. The writer says, " It is getting clearer each year now that these common doctrines of New Buddhism and Christianity were not borrowed from one another, but that both came from a common source, Babylonia." With the question of the " Babylonian " origin of religious ideas we shall deal in our concluding chapter. But here we must remark that it is hardly correct to speak of New (Chinese) Buddhism and Christianity as having either doctrines or origin in common. The writer of the book to which we refer is driven to desperate straits in order to prove his contention. Thus he ventures (in the twentieth century !) to render " Buddha " by " God " : he identifies the Chinese goddess Kwan-yin with the Third Person of the Holy Trinity : and he translates *Tathâgata* (" He who has come as "—others did), one of Buddha's many titles, by " The Incarnate Lord," " The Godlike One," " The Incarnate Transcendent One," and informs his trusting readers that the word would be " best rendered by *Messiah* in English." He then tells us that the book on which he mainly relies (the *Šraddhotpâda Sûtra*) was written by Asvaghosha,

---

[1] Mahâyâna (" Great Vehicle ") Buddhism is the so-called New or Later Buddhism. which arose in Northern India long after Buddha's death and spread thence to China, Tibet, and later to Japan. Southern (or Hînâyâna) Buddhism, as it exists in Ceylon, represents Buddha's teaching far better.

a Sanskrit author of the first Christian century. Now there is probably no Sanskrit scholar who does not deny that this work was written by Ašvaghosha and who does not attribute it to a different writer and a much later age. The Sanskrit original seems no longer to exist, and the Chinese version was made A.D. 554. By such " arguments " as our author uses one may " prove " anything —that the moon is made of green cheese, for example. It is not surprising, therefore, to find that this author concludes that " the Mahâyâna faith is . . . an Asiatic form of the same gospel of our Lord and Saviour Jesus Christ."

A better instance of the unwisdom and the want of logic involved in many of the rash theories of our own age could hardly be found, now that the Baconian theory about the origin of Shakespeare's plays seems to have sunk into the background.[1] It should, however, serve as a warning to those who are interested in Comparative Religion to be careful not to let a perfervid but ill-balanced imagination—their own or any one else's— carry them away. " Prove all things : hold fast that which is good." Not only our own experience but also that of very many enquirers in all ages testifies to the perpetual fulfilment of our Lord's promise, " If any man willeth to DO His will, he shall know of the teaching, whether it be of God, or whether I speak from Myself." [2] Nothing could well be more just than the condition here specified. Knowledge of the Truth does not, and should not, depend upon mere intellectual ability, but upon the

---

[1] But see *The Shakespeare Myth*, by Sir Edwin Durning-Lawrence, 1912.
[2] John vii. 17.

whole-hearted desire to know in order to DO God's will, in a world of deeds, not words, and thus to help in the accomplishment of His glorious and gracious " purpose of the Ages."

[1] Eph. iii. 11.

Contents

CHRISTIANITY AND OTHER FAITHS

CHAPTER I

Religion in General

RELIGION may be defined as belief in some Power (or Powers) superior to man, with which man necessarily stands in some relation of dependence and responsibility, and which is not deaf to prayer and praise.

The number and nature of this Power or these Powers varies infinitely in different religions. In some faiths Polytheism prevails ; for example, in modern Hindûism some thirty-three millions of gods and goddesses are recognized : while Judaism, Christianity and Islâm (Muḥammadanism) are Monotheistic, recognizing only one God. All religions admit the existence of evil Powers as well as of good ; in some, the good are neglected and the evil alone, or almost alone, adored and served. In Zoroastrianism, on the other hand, it was taught that only the good Powers should be worshipped, though in the earlier religion of Persia, in that of Armenia in olden days, and in Mithraism, adoration was offered to both the evil and the good. In modern Hindûism, and in many of the religions of savages, worship and sacrifices are addressed only to evil Powers. Very few religions

consider their gods and goddesses altogether good : most
deities are regarded as strange mixtures of good and evil,
as were those of the ancient Greeks for the most part.
Christianity alone, with its preliminary stage, Judaism,
has the conception of a *Holy* God.   Though some Greek
poets and philosophers reached the conclusion that, if
the gods did evil, they were not really gods at all, yet
their religion taught nothing of the kind.

Many religions recognize three classes of Deities :
(1) The Higher Gods, or the Gods proper ; (2) natural
objects, such as the sun, moon, stars, mountains, rivers,
the earth, the sky, the sea ; (3) the lower Deities, that
is to say, inferior spirits and deified men.   A clear distinction between the first and the third class is drawn
everywhere, or nearly everywhere, in spite of what has
often been said to the contrary.   Zeus in Greece,[1] Jupiter
in Rome, Varuṇa in India, Tangaroa in Polynesia, Unku-
lunkulu among the Zulus, Baiame in Australia, Woden
(Ódhin) among our own northern ancestors, and many
other such deities, were never supposed to have been
men and to have died.   The same statement applies
to deified natural objects.   These were regarded as gods,
probably for several reasons.   Their movements in some
cases, their impassive sublimity in others, seemed to
imply power : and man, conscious of his own personality,
naturally fancied that it existed wherever movement,
sublimity, or any other manifestation of power revealed
itself.   The truth which underlay this conception is,
as we now know, that force ultimately springs from Will
(always, as far as we can judge), and Will implies Mind,
and Mind either Personality or something still *higher*.
Men have been deified after death—and even before

---

[1] In spite of Euhemerus and the Cretan myth.

death—in many parts of the world, as the Pharaohs, the
Cæsars, Romulus, and quite recently Confucius. But
they have always been recognized as holding a place
far inferior [1] to that of the gods proper. Jove and not
Romulus hurled the thunderbolt. To this Osiris in
Egypt *seems* to some to form an exception, but it is not
really so. His name, as we shall see later, is identical
with *Asari*, the Šumerian god of the rising sun, more
commonly known as Marduk, " the good youth " (Merodach). The story of Osiris' murder by his enemy, the
Evil Principle Set, and of his becoming the guide of men
to the Elysian Fields (*Sekhet Åalu* [2]) in the West, where
he reigned over the dead, has probably, therefore, reference to the apparent victory of darkness over the sun in
the evening. This is made still more clear by the fact
that in Egypt Osiris is identified with Rā', the Sun-god,
in hymn after hymn.

The character of the worship and service offered to the
gods varies considerably in different religions. Everywhere something of the nature of prayer and sacrifice
is found, though the former often falls to the level of the
repetition of charms, or to turning the prayer-wheel in
Tibet, and the latter has in nearly every land at some
time or another produced the offering up of human victims—not infrequently the burning alive of little children. Obedience to a large number of minute rules

[1] Thus, according to the *Rig-Veda* (X., 56, 4) the deified
ancestors " have not attained unto the greatness of the gods."
Yama, the first man who died, though later spoken of loosely as
" God of the dead," is in the Rig-Veda distinguished from the
gods.

[2] Erman's method of transliterating Ancient Egyptian is,
no doubt, much more correct than the usual English way, but for
typographical reasons I adopt the latter.

regarding rites and ceremonies, dress, food, habits, even etiquette, in many religions has come to be considered as vastly more important than justice, kindness, purity. In not a few faiths most abominable practices—some of them so vile as to be unmentionable—have been considered necessary to please the gods ; thus in Babylon, Ephesus, throughout Canaan before the Hebrew conquest, and in many other places, religious prostitution was considered not only highly commendable but necessary. It persists to-day in many parts of India. In modern Persia this idea assumes the form of what are called " temporary marriages " at Qum and other " sacred cities." These are, even now, very popular with pilgrims who visit these places to gain merit. Though prohibited by the religious law of the Sunnî Muḥammadans, the practice still flourishes in Mecca itself as well as elsewhere, and was at one time sanctioned by Muhammad.

Mythology is no doubt rightly to be distinguished from religion : yet in many instances we find that the myths which have been associated with the gods have become accepted in their most literal sense, and finally incorporated into the later forms of religions. Many of these stories were no doubt originally devoid of any really very base meaning, being Nature-myths intended to represent the fertilizing power of rain and sunshine, heat and light. Yet when the communities which accepted them grew more and more corrupt, these tales of the gods and goddesses, as Seneca and others have pointed out, became direct incentives to adultery and every form of evil.

In olden days it was among the Israelites alone that God was regarded as " a Power, not ourselves, that makes for righteousness." Old Zoroastrianism tended towards, but never reached, the same conclusion. Among the

Parsîs of the present time, and in a much less degree among the adherents of certain other faiths, something of the same conviction is gradually spreading, owing to Christian influences. Yet there are men of wealth, position, and education in India to-day, who offer mind, property and money (*man, dhan, tan*) in the service of human monsters of abominable wickedness, whom they regard as incarnations of Kṛishṇa, a deity whose whole " history " consists of a carnival of murder, impurity, and filthiness. Religion and morality had very little, if any, connexion with one another among the later Greeks, Romans and Egyptians, though in earlier times they were closely associated together, as in Egypt the " negative confession " in the " Book of the Dead " clearly shows. Yet even the Pyramid Texts speak very strangely of the conduct of the goddess Isis, whose worship had certainly no influence for good when in later times it became popular in Rome. Since Muḥammad's *Hijrah* or " emigration " from Mecca to Medina in A.D. 622, religion and morality can hardly be said to be closely associated in Islâm. Among professing Christians, on the other hand, Antinomianism has only rarely asserted itself openly, and it has then been regarded as a deadly heresy. Wickedness among professing Christians abounds, but always in *opposition* to their religion, not in accordance with it. It is remarkable that, among certain savage tribes in Australia and elsewhere, ethics are a part of religion, and certain forms of vice are strictly prohibited in the name and with the authority of their supreme Deity.

Religions share with everything else on earth the tendency to degeneration and decay. Some are much purer and loftier than others, some are very corrupt indeed.

+ a belief that the moral law is useless.

They differ from one another in very many respects, some sternly prohibiting what others highly commend. Some religions have arisen in historical times, such as Christianity, Islâm, Bahâism, Mormonism ; while others are of immemorial antiquity. Some claim to be intended for all men, others are strictly limited to men of a certain country, or even to certain castes. An almost general rule is, that the further back we trace any religion, the higher are its adherents' ideas of the Divine. Thus in ancient China, as far back as we can go in history, more than 2,000 B.C., Shang-ti, " the Supreme Lord," was adored. Confucius quotes an ancient record which states that the Emperors Wăn and Woo adored Him through sacrifices offered to Heaven and earth. Here we see Nature-worship usurping the place of the earlier worship of God Most High. But often in early times the name Heaven (*T'ien*) was used out of reverence in place of the Divine appellation, as indeed is the case among ourselves occasionally. T'ien was believed to be pleased with good deeds, but to punish wickedness relentlessly. He was placated by the offering of sacrifices. He was feared, but He was not supposed to be the Creator. The spirits of the dead were even then honoured and invoked, but were regarded as quite distinct from T'ien. Adoration is now offered to a host of inferior spirits, often evil ; but Shang-ti, until the end of the Manchu dynasty, was worshipped by the Emperor [1] only, and that too on only one day in each year. Among the Âryans of ancient India, the god Varuṇa (Οὐρανός, Heaven) represented a far higher conception than does any deity now adored by the Hindûs. Ea, " the Lord of deep wisdom," among

---

[1] Probably the President will now discharge this duty.

the Sumerian inhabitants to the north of the Persian Gulf was far superior in character to any of the later deities of Babylon. The same may be said of Rā', the Sun-god, among the Egyptians. He was not their only god, but in the hymns in his honour there occur many passages which show that at times his worshippers looked far beyond the visible sun, and in him, and also in Osiris, adored a by no means unworthy conception of God. Yet later Egyptian religion thought more of the Bull Apis (*Ḥâpi*), the cat-headed goddess Bast, the heifer Isis, and such-like—at least in the practical worship and belief of the people—than of any such lofty idealizations. "The sublimer portions of the Egyptian religion are not the comparatively late result of a process of development. The sublimer portions are demonstrably ancient, and the last stage of the Egyptian religion was by far the grossest and most corrupt," as Professor Renouf says.

Civilization often degrades religion, rendering it formal, superstitious, unreal; putting rites and ceremonies in the place of spirituality and sincerity. The tendency is to forget God, to leave worship to a certain privileged class, and thus to let it be crowded out of practical life. Even Christianity is liable to corruption in this way. History shows, also, that many heathen ideas and practices have crept into certain sections of the Church. Examples of these are saint and image-worship, the use of holy water, Mariolatry, and other practices alien to the teaching of the New Testament. A still more dangerous tendency at the present day is to drift away from everything positive and distinctive in Christianity, and to substitute for it, though without change of name, a nondescript form of Deism, or an indefinite Unitarian-

ism. At one time Christendom became almost polytheistic, it may now become practically Atheistic, unless
this universal tendency to corruption is checked in time,
as it has been more than once in the history of the Christian Church. Our own experience of such tendencies
in Christianity enables us to understand how non-Christian faiths also, in both ancient and modern times, have
lost their purity and admitted manifold forms of corruption. In exactly the same way Vedic Hindûism yielded
gradually to Brâhmaṇical sacerdotalism in one direction
and to an agnostic and pantheistic philosophy in the
other, until it lost almost every vestige of truth and
became the degraded system of pantheistic polytheism
which prevails in India to-day. The facts of history and
experience, therefore, are opposed to the modern popular
theory that religion has steadily progressed in purity
and spirituality from early ages to the present day.

CHAPTER II

Religion and Religions : Universality of Religion

THE various religions of the world differ so much from one another that the favourite modern and pseudo-liberal idea that they all mean very much the same thing, that all alike lead in different ways to the same goal—a purely Hindû view, by the way—is entirely due to ignorance and carelessness. Of course they have some points in common with one another, since they are *religions*, not philosophies. In a sense, it may be said that they have the same aim, because they all seek to please the Deity or deities whom they acknowledge. They have certain tenets in common, such as belief in an After-life of some kind ; though these common beliefs are much fewer than they are often said to be. But, on the other hand, the differences between the various religions of the world regarding the nature of the Deity, and concerning the worship which should be offered to Him, are abysmal. People nowadays speak as if the fact that all religions alike aim at the attainment of salvation in some sense made it a matter of indifference to which a man belongs, provided he is in earnest—as most of those who speak in this way are not—in religious matters. There are two fallacies here which should be exposed.

As to oneness of aim : we must not forget that the medi-
eval method of pouring boiling oil into gunshot wounds
had exactly the same goal in view as has our modern
aseptic method of treatment, yet it would hardly be a
matter of indifference to our readers, if suffering from
bullet wounds, which of the two systems was adopted
in their own case, nor would the result be the same.
Earnestness again is a very good thing in what is right,
but the same feeling applied to what is wrong is perhaps
less admirable.   " There still exist in parts of America,"
says Charles Reade,[1] " rivers on whose banks are earnest
men, who shall take your scalp, the wife's of your bosom,
and the innocent child's of her bosom."   Such earnestness does not, however, in our eyes, justify these men's
conduct : nor does the same quality render praiseworthy
the rites and practices of certain religions, such as some
we have already mentioned, or, again, like those of the
Aztecs of Mexico, whose priests used to cut open with
obsidian knives the breasts of human victims laid on the
stone of slaughter in the temple of the god Huitzilopochtli,
tear out their hearts, and burn them when still palpitating
before the idol, afterwards holding a sacred feast on the
bodies.   In the non-Christian world even now, in the
name of religion, still worse things happen.

The study of Comparative Religion as a whole, and
of the individual faiths of men of every age, race and
clime, is of interest and importance for many reasons.
In the first place it testifies to the immense difference
between truth and falsehood in religion : and in the
second it bears witness to the universality of religion,
and consequently to man's consciousness that he needs
a faith of some kind, and will hold a bad religion if he

[1] *Christie Johnstone*, chap. ix.

cannot get a good one,—sometimes even in preference to the latter.

For Anthropology has taught us the universality of religion in some form or other. Again and again travellers have asserted that they had discovered tribes destitute of anything of the sort, but in each case fuller knowledge has enabled us to correct their mistake. It has possibly arisen from the absence of temples and even of images and fetishes among certain savages, as for instance in Australia and among the Maoris of New Zealand. Yet enquiry has revealed among some aboriginal tribes in Australia very lofty and even spiritual conceptions of the Divine, and in some cases an approach to Monotheism. At least one tribe calls their Supreme Deity, " Our Father in the Sky," and believes that He punishes breaches of the moral laws which He has given. The corrupt religions of certain highly civilized nations have sometimes lost sight of any real connexion between faith and morals, and have even enjoined immoral conduct ; but originally this cannot have been so, and was not so, as far as history guides us. " Without a code of morals," says Dr. Tylor,[1] " the very existence of the rudest tribe would be impossible ; and indeed the moral standards of even savage tribes are to no small extent well defined and praiseworthy." [2] This must have been true in the earliest times as well as the present. It is impossible to conceive of any form of social life—and man is a social being—without some system of ethics. Even at the present day every attempt to give effect to any ethical system among a community, without religion,

---

[1] *Primitive Culture*, vol. ii., p. 360.

[2] So Hegel says, " Morality is the substance of society ; religion is the substance of morality."

has failed. It is still true that " you cannot make men moral by Act of Parliament."

A modern French writer on religion tells us that it is through the religious feeling that the human species has been able to raise itself above the other animals. [1] " It has been, in a word, the civilizing faculty of Humanity. If it did not determine the formation of the earliest societies, it has been the means of their preservation and progress." He enquires how could young and newly-formed communities have continued to exist in primitive times, had not religion brought to the aid of political, moral, economic and even hygienic laws the warnings of punishment and the promises of reward at the hands of some superhuman Power. Leaving entirely aside the teaching of Holy Scripture on this subject, we learn from archæology the existence of religion in the earliest times of which any remains have been found. Altars, the relics of sacrifices, the burial of articles with the dead, charms, amulets, and countless other objects testify to this. The ancients firmly believed in the universality of religion, and found it wherever they went. " You may see states without walls, without laws, without coins, without writing ; but a people without a god, without worship, without religious practices and sacrifices, hath no man seen," says Plutarch.[2] Modern discoveries abundantly confirm this. Even when an atheistic system of philosophy, like Buddhism, has for a time prevailed, it has ultimately been developed into a religious system, as in Tibet and Burma : for religion is a necessity—as even Herbert Spencer admits

[1] A. de Molinari, *Religion*, p. 178.
[2] *Adv. Colotem Epicureum.*

in his Autobiography,—at least under present conditions. A distinguished Anthropologist says :—

> I have looked for Atheism with the greatest care. I have met with it nowhere except as an erratic condition among some philosophical sects belonging to the most anciently civilized nations. If we accept as well founded the statements of some travellers, perhaps it exists besides among a very small number of isolated and little-known tribes, among which the constant requirements of a miserable existence have stifled every other consideration. But it is clear that extremely rare and always much restricted exceptions do not invalidate the generality of the basal fact, any more than the colour-blindness of certain individuals invalidates that of the part which our eye plays in the perception of colours. . . . No large human race, no widespread population, not a fraction, however unimportant, of these races or populations is atheistic. [1]

It is not too much to say with Plato that religion is the chief thing which distinguishes man from brute. Tennyson is merely stating a scientific fact when he puts into the mouth of the dying King Arthur the well known lines :—

> For what are men better than sheep or goats
> That nourish a blind life within the brain,
> If, knowing God, they lift not hands of prayer
> Both for themselves and those who call them friend ?
> For so the whole round earth is every way
> Bound by gold chains about the feet of God.

The last two lines, in fact, express what, in the opinion of many ancient authorities, and some modern, was the idea which gave birth to the very name of " Religion." [2]

The fact of the universality of religion is a very striking proof of its truth, in the sense that evidently man uni-

---

[1] De Quatrefages, *Introduction à l'étude des races humaines,* p. 255.

[2] As derived from *religare,* " to bind."

versally requires a religion of some kind and acknowledges quite naturally and spontaneously that the presupposi- tions common to all religions are facts. These presup- positions which the existence of religion in all ages and among all races shows to be assumed by men in general as axioms are : (1) The existence of some superior Power or Powers to whom man is responsible ; (2) the difference between right and wrong ; and (3) the fact of an After- life. For these beliefs lie at the root of all religion. Universality of any conviction is, in the opinion of Aris- totle, Cicero, and Hooker, a proof of the truth of that conviction. This view is well expressed by Hooker [1] : " The general and perpetual voice of men is as the sentence of God Himself. For that which all men have at all times learned, Nature herself must needs have taught ; and God being the Author of Nature, her voice is but His instrument." Only in this sense is the saying true, " Vox Populi vox Dei."

It may seem a strange thing to say, but it is none the less a fact, that there could be no such thing as religion were not religion in some form true. The very exist- ence of religion as an universal fact proves that it rests upon some great Reality. This follows from considering the lesson taught us by each of our faculties. Every one of them corresponds to some outside *reality*, and testifies to the existence of its object. Thus, for example, the fact that we have the faculty of sight proves that there is something to see. Of course, no absolutely con- clusive proof has ever been given, nor perhaps will ever be given, that the external world exists, that its apparent existence is not due to our imagination. But the proofs

[1] *Ecc. Polity*, Bk. I, ch. viii., § 3.

that there is an external world are sufficiently convincing for most of us, except philosophical Hindûs. So with hearing and our other faculties. The fact that we possess the auditory sense is a proof that sound is not altogether a delusion. Feeling shows that there do exist tangible objects. So also ability to think proves that there is something to think about. Just in the same way the faculty of adoration proves that there really does exist an object of worship—nay more, a *worthy* object of worship. If the religious instinct—for it is an instinct—were found only in a few persons, it would prove nothing very much : but its universality, or all but universality,[1] is of itself a conclusive evidence of the existence of its object, God. For the religious instinct is at least as universal as hearing and sight. The existence of a few blind or deaf people does not affect the argument, for it is beyond question that these are not normal men. The physically perfect and normal man does possess hearing and sight. The existence of a comparatively small number of people who do not seem to possess the religious faculty does not render nugatory the statement that normally this faculty belongs to man as man. No blind, no deaf, no atheistic tribe has as yet been found, and the probability of such being discovered grows less day by day. But, if our travellers were some day to find, in Central Africa or Borneo perhaps, a blind tribe of men, would that disprove the fact that the normal man possesses sight, or the argument that, therefore, there is

[1] In the *Protagoras* (ch. xii.), Plato represents that philosopher, with Socrates' assent, as holding that religion and morals were known to men as *men*, because of their affinity with the gods, even before they had learned to use speech, houses, or clothes,

something in the world around us to see, some reality corresponding to the all-but-universal sense of sight? In just the same way, how would the oft-asserted but never-proved existence of a tribe devoid of all religious ideas demonstrate the futility of the argument based on man's possession of the religious faculty in general?

The religious faculty may be misused : so may sight and hearing. It may be turned aside to unworthy objects, as the other faculties too often are. It may become dull or atrophied, just as is often the case with the visual and auditory faculties. When this degeneration takes place, it often manifests itself in the form of a firm belief in " luck," or in unswerving reliance upon a " mascot " of some sort. These are really phenomena of great scientific interest. They are the forms which the lowest intellectual degeneration of the religious faculty assumes among ourselves, and they closely correspond to belief in fetishes among negroes of a low type. A man who scoffs at or neglects Christianity but cherishes a " lucky sixpence " is nevertheless a religious man in a way. He has the religious faculty as well as any one else. He has but exchanged belief in the Living God for belief in the omniscience and almightiness of a coin. Others prefer a cat or a dog as the object of their deep superstitious reliance, in this imitating in form the ancient Egyptians, though differing from them in lacking all the deeper idealism which perhaps to some extent in the minds of the philosophers of Egypt formed an excuse for such degradation of the human before the bestial. But the existence of such phenomena in our day explains their occurrence in earlier times.

There are many different theories of the origin of religion. Our age is great in theories. We cannot now discuss those connected with the supposed source [1] from which religion sprang ; but, on whatever theory, the result for our present purpose is the same. Religion is a fact. As such it has to be accounted for. Its very existence shows that man is conscious of needs higher than earth alone can satisfy. Even on the evolutionary theory, some great purpose must underly its evolution, just as much at least as that of sight, hearing, or any other faculty. In whatever way religion came into existence, there can be no question that it has developed stage by stage, although with many terrible relapses. Only in one single family and nation can it be said, in fact, that religion has really advanced at all from primitive times. Elsewhere its history, wherever it can be traced, is a melancholy story of steady progress downwards, of the gradual degradation of the idea of the Divine, of the separation of religion from morality—in too many cases resulting in its becoming the pander to the lowest vices that disgrace humanity. Yet in that one nation and in its spiritual heirs there has been steady advance in religious conceptions and growth in the knowledge of what God must be. Hence it is clear that, if humanity is ever to find a religion suitable for all alike, true, and worthy of both God and man, it must be in the one line in which spiritual progress has been made and in which a Divine plan for the religious education of the race has been continuously carried out age by age.

Hegel, in his philosophic way, speaks of three stages of religion, comparing them with the three chief periods of human life. First, he places the religions of nature,

---

[1] I may perhaps be permitted to refer to my *Comparative Religion* (Longmans), ch. i., where such theories are considered.

comparing their time to that of the childhood of humanity. Then come the religions of spirituality, which he compares to youth. Thirdly, he places what he terms the Absolute Religion (i.e., Christianity), calling this the religion of the manhood of our race. If this comparison has any value, then Fetishism and Atheism would represent slightly varied forms of the senility or second childhood of mankind. There is a theory that man will ultimately outgrow religion. Well, in old age people sometimes " outgrow " their senses and their intellect. A very painful sight this is, but much more painful is it to see even a small section of the human race in senility in religious matters, devoting itself to pleasure, as old men in the Panjâb often take to flying kites from the roof-top —a game which sometimes leads to their falling to the ground and breaking their necks. Money-grubbing, like that of the " man with the muck-rake " in *Pilgrim's Progress*, is a no less painful and saddening sign of the senility of the race, or rather of a part of it. We may well be thankful for the assurance that, if loss of interest in all religion is really a sign of the advancing senility of humanity, its second childhood is as yet far off, judging by the immense interest the subject still excites. " Religion is neither dead nor dying," says Naville: " of this I need no proof beyond the trouble which so many people are taking to kill it." Goethe well writes : " The only real and the deepest theme of the world's and of man's history, to which all other matters are subordinate, is the conflict between faith and unbelief."

Nothing in the whole history of the world has influenced men more powerfully, for good or for evil, than religion —using the word in the sense already defined. When at its best it has produced the noblest self-devotion and heroism, lives of which "the world was not worthy," hospitals, reformatories, a pure and lofty morality, peace in life and hope in death. Among its fruits in the individual are "love, peace, gentleness, goodness, faith, meekness, temperance." On the other hand, in its corrupt forms it has given birth to bigotry, cruel and sensual superstitions, abject bondage to a priesthood, slavery to terror in both life and death, persecutions, human sacrifices, inhuman tortures, *autos-da-fé*, the Inquisition, the horrors committed by the orders of the "Old Man of the Mountain" in olden times and by those of a Sultan styled "the Murderer" in our own days, religious wars, massacres, immorality of nearly every imaginable kind, rendering men demons or swine. Evidently, then, the immensity of the power, for good or for bad, possessed and exercised by religion cannot be ignored or denied by any one who is even in the slightest degree acquainted with the history of any single country in the world. It is possible, therefore, to speak of religion as the greatest blessing to humanity, or as its greatest curse ; but in each case we are stating only a half-truth, and a half-truth is often the worst of all lies. The better a thing is, the worse it becomes if abused. We see this in the case of food, fire, electricity, and many other things, including kingly or other rule. Opium is invaluable as an anaesthetic and a medicine ; but the very qualities which render it so potent for good make it equally potent for evil. So it is with religion, as all experience shows. Hence we see the folly of those who in our own day think it a sign of their superior knowledge and breadth of mind to say that one religion is as good as another, that we should never try to " proselytise " or in any way to alter any man's religious convictions, that it does not at all matter what a man's belief is, so long as his conduct is right, and so on. If a man's professed belief does not affect his conduct for good or for evil, then it is not his real belief at all. Belief is conviction, and as such cannot possibly exist without showing itself in action. It is just because religion affects, and must affect, both character and conduct that it has always played such a vitally important part in the history of the world.

A mighty stream like the Hoang-Ho, the Yang-tse-Kiang, or the Euphrates, may bring fertility to vast tracts of land and provide food for millions of men, or it may turn millions of square miles into unhealthy marshes, or sweep away myriads of human beings in flood after flood. The one impossible thing is for it to produce no effect, good or bad. So with religion and the religious instinct. A great force of this kind cannot be put aside, and by no wise man will such a force be regarded as a negligible quantity. That it has frequently been wrongly used proves that it may and should be used aright, and its efficacy for good should be employed to the utmost. If not so employed, it must continue to do mischief, for it cannot be eradicated from humanity as a whole. If it were, man would no longer be man, as we have already seen.

It is clear then that it is most important to discriminate between true and false religion. St. Paul's advice on this point is consonant with reason and common sense : " Prove all things ; hold fast that which is good." In this matter witnesses of all kinds may be called, but after all conscience is the judge for each of us. Only we must be sure not to mistake for conscience a judgment warped by prejudice or self-interest,

" Commodity the bias of the world."

We must, of course, first make sure that we rightly understand the doctrines of the religion which we bring before the bar of conscience.   Men do not often do this, strange as it may seen.   Herbert Spencer, for instance, thinker as he was, in his Autobiography tells us that even quite early in life he condemned Christianity because, as he held, it taught certain doctrines.   He mentions a whole list of these.   It is not too much to say that he would have been justified, *in foro conscientiae*, in rejecting Christianity, *if* it taught such tenets as those he details.   But *not one* of them is inculcated in Holy Scripture, the one authoritative source of the Christian faith.   On the other hand, men in this country sometimes accept—or at least for a time profess great admiration for—Buddhism, Islâm, Bahâism, without any real knowledge of what these systems teach.   Again, it is a very rare thing indeed, even among educated people, to find the knowledge that such things as " Christian Evidences " exist.   What these Evidences in general are it is not our present business to enquire, though before the end of this book our readers will be able to judge whether the new Science of Comparative Religion forms one of them or not.   If God has spoken unto men in answer to the appeal of the religious faculty, which He has made the most important and the highest part of our being, then there can be no question that His answer must possess unmistakable proofs of its Divine origin and authority, if we have ears to hear and hearts to understand.

CHAPTER III

An Attempted Classification of Religions

MANY attempts have been made to classify religions
under different heads, but it can hardly be said
that any one of them has become generally recognized
as satisfactory in all respects.

One of these systems of classification would divide
religions into two classes : (1) " Book Religions," and
(2) those devoid of an authoritative sacred literature.
Perhaps the only " Book Religions " of any importance
are the Ancient Egyptian, the Assyrio-Babylonian, the
Hebrew, the Christian, Islâm, Hindûism, Buddhism
(Northern and Southern, or Mahâyâna and Hînâyâna),
Sikhism, Japanese Shintoism, and Taouism. Confucianism is as much a philosophy as Platonism, and cannot
be counted as a religion. The same is true of *original*
Buddhism, but later Buddhism has developed into several
different religions. To " Book Religions," might perhaps
be added Mormonism, Bahâism, " Christian Science "
and Theosophy. But this division, though somewhat
convenient, has nothing scientific about it, being founded
upon a mere contingency.

To divide religions into ancient and modern, or living
and dead, would not do, because in one sense no religion
has ever in reality died out. Take, for instance, that of
the ancient Egyptians. Not only has much of it been

traced among their modern descendants, whether Coptic Christians or Muslims, but it is admitted that some statues and pictures of the Virgin and Child have been in large measure borrowed from Egyptian representations of Isis and the infant Horus.   To the worship of Isis and Ishtar (Ashtoreth, Astartê), her equivalent Asian Nature-goddess, a good deal of Mariolatry may be traced back. The title " Queen of Heaven " was a very early Sumerian appellation of Ishtar.   In the same way primitive Animism, or belief in a great number of Spirits everywhere present, may be said to survive in modern Hindûism, in the *Nat*-worship of Burmese Buddhists, in the ancient religion of Egypt, and in the worship of trees and the honour paid to the famous Black Stone in the wall of Ka'bah at Mecca by professing Muslims.   Saint-worship among both Muslims and Christians, and the adoration paid to sacred images and pictures among some of the latter, are distinct survivals of ancient polytheism.   English, German, Scandinavian and Russian superstitions are perhaps in every case due to the same thing—such as bowing to the new moon, hanging the horseshoe over the door, or fearing to sit down thirteen in company—the latter probably a reminiscence of the slaying of Baldr the Beautiful, when all the Twelve Gods were assembled along with Loki, the Evil Principle, who was descended from the wicked Giants.[1]   " Popular Christianity " often shows a good deal of underlying heathenism, not only in its retention of such words as " lucky " and " unlucky," but also in some common but utterly unscriptural theories of Atonement and of God's ways of dealing with His creatures.   In the same way many ancient Arabian be-

[1] The popular idea that the superstition is connected with the number present at the Last Supper seems unfounded.

liefs are perpetuated in Islâm. Ṣûfîism, and its modern development Bahâism, also contain much that is of Hindû origin.

The division into true and false is also unsatisfactory, for some truth is to be found in all religions, though often *buried* rather than set forth or contained in them, or so distorted and mixed with falsehood as to be productive of harm by tending to commend the errors with which it is overlaid. Thus in Islâm we find the great truth of the Oneness of God, in Buddhism belief in the enduring consequences of good and bad actions done here on earth (the doctrine of *Karma*), and so on. The false, too, is found in all religions, in one sense ; for, as we have seen, a good deal of heathenism survives in some popular unscriptural views entertained in certain forms of Christianity itself. Elsewhere we often find evil deeds enjoined and good ones condemned. For example, the Afghân Ghâzî believes that, as a zealous Muslim, it is a virtuous deed for him to kill a Christian, all the more so if he sacrifices his own life thereby. The Ṭhags in India used to murder travellers in order to propitiate the goddess Kâlî. On the other hand, the Jains deem it as wrong to kill a mosquito as a human being. Though all religions recognize a distinction between right and wrong, yet in most cases there is great confusion in deciding what is right and what should be condemned as wrong.

A division of some value is that into National and Universal religions. The former are religions which belong exclusively to one tribe or nation, and do not claim the allegiance of any one not of that tribe. Most religions of the ancient world were of this class. Often the religion belonged rather to the country than to the people. A Babylonian's gods were not able to save him from the lions if he settled in Samaria : he had, therefore, he thought, to learn the " manner [1] of the God of the land." A Hindû, on the contrary, may build temples to his gods in South Africa, but (strictly speaking) people of any other blood than his own, people whose ancestors were not Hindûs, ought not to be admitted into his religion—though arrangements are now made for permitting this in certain cases.   Universal religions are those which lay claim to dominion over the whole human race.   The only universal religions in this sense are Buddhism, Christianity and Islâm, to which we may now perhaps add Bahâism, an offshoot from an Islâmic sect, but one which is largely Pantheistic (and very intolerant in reality, though pretending the contrary).   People who profess a National religion or tribal creed admit that the religions of other nations or tribes are quite correct for members of those nations, though not for themselves.   Thus the Greek and the Egyptian each regarded with respect the religion of the other ; and it is said that the Emperor Alexander Severus wished to admit our Lord into the Roman Pantheon, and to build a temple to Him.[2]   But the Muslim believes that the Christian is utterly wrong and is " among those that are lost."   The Christian knows that " there is no other Name under Heaven, given among men," except the Name of the Lord Jesus Christ, whereby men can come to the true knowledge of God and become heirs of salvation.   Each universal religion is bound to endeavour to spread throughout the world and to become in reality, as in claim, the creed of the whole human race.

Here we may mention Hegel's division of religions

[1] With 2 Kings xvii. 27, cf. Naaman's request in 2 Kings v. 17.
[2] *Lampridius*, cap. 43.

into two classes, (1) the Absolute Religion, which is Christianity, and (2) all other faiths. There is much to be said for this classification, for undoubtedly Christianity cannot be put into the same class with any other faith without ignoring what is most distinctive about it. Christianity has points of contact, so to speak, with all other religions ; it has resemblances to some other faiths—though these have been much exaggerated by certain writers of our own day—it stands in some relation (to be considered later) with them all. Yet the vast and essential differences between the Christian and all other religions are such that the attempt to put it into the same category with any other faith argues a want of discrimination, due perhaps to lack of knowledge of the other religions which it is thought to resemble. We shall see later in what such resemblances as have been pointed out between Christianity and certain other faiths consist, as far as they have any existence except in the imagination. But in this very important matter scientific investigation is necessary, together with painstaking accuracy, precision and earnestness. Writers on this subject should beware of having

> The poet's eye, in a fine frenzy rolling,

for it is still true that

> As imagination bodies forth
> The forms of things unknown, the poet's pen
> Turns them to shapes, and gives to airy nothings
> A local habitation and a name.

Leaving, therefore, real or fancied resemblances between Christianity [1] and other religions for later consideration, we must here point out a few matters in which the differ-

---

[1] Including, its earlier stage, Biblical Judaism.

ence is so great as to justify Hegel in putting Christianity into a category apart from all others as the Absolute Religion. Among others, the following points present themselves :

1. No other religion has any distinctive evidences, or can be said to be based on definite historical facts which can be tested.

2. No other reveals a God of *Holiness*,[1] a Deity worthy of being worshipped in the twentieth century, neither " outgrown " nor likely to be outgrown.

3. No other faith appeals to and works through so lofty a motive-power and one which is the very highest imaginable, love to God because of the conviction of His love towards us.

4. No other faith has even tended to produce such practical good results, moral, physical, intellectual, social, spiritual.

5. No other religion enables each of its earnest adherents to attain to a personal knowledge of God, as distinct from the real or supposed knowledge of doctrines *about* God. Christianity displays the one perfect human character as at once our example and " the image of the Invisible God," who is seen in Him and in Him alone.

6. Christianity alone displays sin in its true heinousness and deadliness, and at the same time offers deliverance from the love, the power, and the eternal consequences of sin.

7. Christianity alone gives inward peace, satisfies man's spiritual yearnings, and has proved itself equally well adapted in this and other respects to all nations of

---

[1] Islâm, though it borrows the title *Al Quddûs* (" the Holy ") for God from Judaism, most emphatically *does not* regard Him as a morally Holy Being.

men, thus alone showing itself capable of becoming the religion of the whole human race.

8. Christianity has all, and more than all, the good and none of the evil found in other religions.

Thus, looked at even from its human side, it is evident that the Christian faith is the Absolute Religion as being the keystone of the arch, the complement of men's feeling after God, the ultimate goal towards which all that is best and truest in all other faiths has always unswervingly tended, thus enabling us to recognize a Divine plan in the religious education of the human race.

CHAPTER IV

Christianity in its Relation to all Other Faiths

IN our own time a great deal has been written upon this subject, and very rightly so, for it is of primary importance. The whole question of the origin, the truth, the historicity, the authority of Christianity, is bound up with it. In the present chapter we can deal with only certain aspects of the matter, and that somewhat briefly, contenting ourselves with a fuller treatment of the most important points in subsequent chapters.

I. According to one view, the Christian religion stands on exactly the same footing as all others, being a somewhat confused and disguised form of Nature-religion, misunderstood by its own first propagators. Some years ago, when the famous Sun-myth theory was " the latest thing out," and was—by many people—considered as one of the greatest discoveries of the nineteenth century, our Lord Jesus Christ was said to be merely another form of the Sun-god, as were Buddha, Krishna, Mithra, and other " Divine Saviours." Much curious learning and a vast deal of brilliant imaginative power were devoted to proving this ingenious hypothesis. Men were reminded that the twelve apostles meant the twelve months in the year, or the twelve chief signs of the Zodiac ; that

Apollo, the Sun-god, was born in a miraculous manner ; that Attis, another Sun-god, was said to have come to life again ; that the Sun-god Osiris rose from the dead ; that the Sun-god Tammuz descended to the lower world ; and so on *ad infinitum*. All this was answered—partly by anticipation—by Archbishop Whately in his clever " Historic Doubts [1] relative to Napoleon Buonaparte," written in reply to Hume's " Essay on Miracles," and more recently by a French writer,[2] who reduced the theory to the absurd by showing that the Sun-god Myth theory would apply far better to Napoleon Buonaparte.[3] We may condense the argument in the following way :

Napoleon is clearly an impersonation of the sun, as will be evident from the considerations which we here present.

(1) Napoleon = Apollo, the Sun-god, for on a column in the Place Vendôme his name is spelled Néapoléo, evidently from the Greek *nê* or *nai*, the affirmative particle, and *Apollo*, meaning " the very Apollo, or Sun."

---

[1] *The Pamphleteer*, vol. xxvii., London, 1821.

[2] Vide Rev. S. Baring-Gould's *Curious Myths of the Middle Ages*, pp. 127, *sqq.*

[3] Dealing with the attempt to explain away the histories of historical persons as " Sun-myths," Dr. Tylor shows that " the life of Julius Cæsar would fit . . . plausibly into a scheme of solar myth : his splendid course as in each new land he came and saw and conquered ; his desertion of Cleopatra ; his ordinance of the solar year for men ; his death at the hand of Brutus, like Sifrit's death at the hand of Hagen in the Nibelungen Lied ; his falling, pierced with many bleeding wounds, and shrouding himself in his cloak to die in darkness. Of Cæsar, better than of Cassius his slayer, it might have been said, in the language of sun-myth :—

> . . . . . . O setting sun,
> As in thy red rays thou dost smite to-night,
> So in his red blood Cassius' day is set,
> The sun of Rome is set ! "
>
> (Tylor, *Primitive Culture*, 4th ed., vol. i.,
> pp. 319, 320.)

(2) The surname *Buona-parte* proves this, for the sun rules the day, the " good part " of the twenty-four hours.

(3) The myth says that Apollo was born at Delos, a Mediterranean island. Napoleon was also born in a Mediterranean island, Corsica. Pausanias styles Apollo an Egyptian deity. The Napoleonic myth states that the people of Egypt paid homage to Napoleon.

(4) Napoleon's mother was named *Lætitia*, which means " joy," evidently referring to the dawning light and the deepening joy of Nature, bursting into song and delight at the daily birth of the sun. Apollo's mother's name was Lêto : but *læto*, the active form of *lætor*, " to rejoice," means " to cause to rejoice," and *lætitia* comes from it.

(5) Napoleon had three graceful sisters, as had Apollo, whose sisters were the three Graces.

(6) Napoleon in the myth has four brothers, evidently the four seasons. Three become actual kings, because Spring, Summer and Autumn reign respectively over flowers, harvest, and fruit. The seasons owe all to the sun, as Napoleon's brothers in the myth owed all to him. One of them was not really a king, because Winter reigns over no produce. If it be urged that Winter rules over frost, this confirms what has been said, for, *when Napoleon's power was declining*, when the allied armies invaded France (that is to say, when the boreal blasts swept over the earth), his fourth brother was given the rule of *Canino* (from *cani*, " *hoary* hairs," referring to the *hoar*-frosts of winter, as the poet says :

cum gelidus crescit *canis* in montibus humor.)

The Northern Powers displace the many-coloured flag (the *tricoleur*) in favour of the white standard of the

D

Bourbons—that is, the powerful north winds drive the colours from the landscape and cover it with snow.

(7) In the myth, Napoleon had two wives. So had Apollo : for Plutarch tells us that the Greeks gave him the moon as his spouse, the Egyptians the earth. By the moon he had no son, but by the earth he became father of the younger Horus. The latter denotes the fruit of the field produced by the sun's genial influence. The son of the mythic Napoleon was born on March 20, the season of the Spring equinox, when agriculture is becoming active.

(8) Napoleon freed France from " the hydra of revolution." Apollo released Hellas from the Python. " Revolution," from *revolvo*, evidently refers to the *coils* of a serpent.

(9) Napoleon is said to have had twelve Marshals at the head of his armies, and four others stationary. The latter are of course the four Cardinal points, while the former are the Zodiacal signs, marching under the sun's orders, each commanding a host of stars.

(10) The mythic Napoleon victoriously traversed the south, but failed when he tried to penetrate the north. The sun's power is greater in the south, but it goes north after the Spring equinox, and *after three months' march* it is driven back, following Cancer. Hence comes the mythic account of Napoleon's march towards Moscow and his retreat with great loss.

(11) Finally, the sun rises in the east and sets in the western sea, after reigning in the sky for twelve hours. Napoleon in the myth rose in a Mediterranean island, ruled for twelve years, and vanished in the Atlantic.

This exceedingly able skit, if we may so style it, completely explodes the Sun-myth theory with reference to all historical personages. It is also a warning to men not to be led astray by many very plausible modern hypotheses, such as not a few[1] indulged in by even able writers on Comparative Religion who are opposed to Christianity. If any system of argument is such that by it one may prove Napoleon's whole career to be but a Solar myth (though some of our grandfathers fought against him at Waterloo—unless they too were Solar myths !), then it is safe to conclude that there is *some* flaw in the argument, however plausible it may seem, and that it is unsafe to rely upon it in other cases, too. This is a general rule. It is unnecessary to deal further with the Sun-myth theory, for, though once advocated by very able writers, it may now be said to be completely exploded in its *original* form.

In a disguised form, however, the same theory is being continually revived for the benefit of those who are not quite up-to-date in matters of modern speculation. Not a few books are in active circulation still, which try to prove that what the Gospels teach about Christ was taught ages before His appearance regarding others, such as Attis, Osiris, Adonis, Mithra (all of whom are undoubtedly Sun-gods). Of course this is not true, but that is a mere detail. When facts cannot be distorted into the form required, then imagination is called in, and such terms as " we must assume," " no doubt," " in all probability," have to fill up gaps in the line of argument. It is unfortunately true that some writers have deliberately en-

---

[1] E.g., Dr. Frazer's theory that the Biblical account of our Lord's mocking, scourging, and crucifixion may be derived from some imaginary Sacæe-festival *at Jerusalem.* His strongest " proofs " are " perhaps," " in the absence of positive information, we may conjecture," etc., etc.

deavoured to deceive people by relating tales about Krishna and Buddha, for example, which are not found in any Oriental work whatever, though these writers venture to quote some Sanskrit books by name as their authority,[1] trusting to the widespread credulity about, and ignorance of, Oriental faiths which still prevail in Europe and America. Here again the motto, " Prove all things ; hold fast that which is good," should be taken as our guide.

That the great majority of religions have confounded God with the powers of Nature is only too true. We are in danger of doing the same thing ourselves, and often do so. But it does not follow from this that Buddha, Zoroaster, Confucius were originally Nature-powers personified, any more than Manes, Muhammad, or Mrs. Eddy. Men in Carlyle's opinion were " mostly fools," but hardly such fools as all that.

II. Another theory is that Christianity is an eclectic religion, having (consciously or unconsciously) borrowed a very great deal from previous faiths and philosophies. Writers in support of this view sometimes endeavour to prove that Christianity is Mithraism in another form. Others think most of it has come from Buddhism. Others assert that the Doctrine of the Trinity was undoubtedly

---

[1] Thus E. Schuré, *Krishna and Orpheus*, Eng. translation, professes to draw his statements from the *Vishnu Purâna* and the *Bhagavad-Gîtâ* (p. 10). Yet the whole book is a mass of utterly shameless lying, as any Orientalist will avouch. The author's learning is not equal to his mendacity, cf. his derivation of *poetry* ($\pi o i \eta \sigma \iota s$) " from the Phœnician *phohe* (mouth, voice, language, speech) and *ish* (Superior Being, principal Being, figuratively God)," etc., etc. (p. 100, note).

Another writer of the same class is M. Jacolliot, whose book, *La Bible dans l'Inde et La Vie de Jezeus Christna* has been ably exposed by Prof. de Harlez, *Védisme, Brahmanisme et Christianisme*.

taken from the Hindû doctrine of the *Trimûrti*. Yet another body of investigators asserts that it came from Egypt. The doctrine of the Resurrection has by some been traced to Persia, by others with equal confidence to Egypt. Confucius is declared to have taught the Golden Rule centuries before Christ. Here, again, when we put such assertions to the proof, their want of foundation becomes evident. Some of the points we have just mentioned will require full consideration later, but others may be dealt with at once. With regard to the *Trimûrti* or " Three-formed," a triad representing the group of *three separate* Hindû Gods, Brahmâ, Vishṇu and Šiva, it will be enough to quote a couple of leading Orientalists' opinions, or rather conclusions, on the point. The celebrated Italian Professor, Angelo de Gubernatis, speaks of it as " This late Brâhmaṇical, or rather Purâṇic conception, imitated from the Christian doctrine disfigured." [1] Professor de Harlez quotes this statement with approval as in complete agreement with his own view, and adds, " This adoption, this invention, does not go back further than the beginning of the Middle Ages. The word *trimûrti* is modern and little used." [2] As to the correctness of this view there can be no doubt, even if it be not regarded as certain that the Indian Triad was derived from a misunderstanding of the Christian doctrine of the Trinity.

When we turn to Egypt we find nothing at all corresponding to this Christian doctrine. What the Egyptians themselves had not, assuredly they could not lend to others. The doctrine of the Trinity is that the Divine Unity exists in three Hypostases. Now in Egypt we

[1] *Enciclopedia indica,* p. 363.
[2] *Védisme, Brahmanisme, et Christianisme,* p. 112.

find Triads, that is, groups or families of three separate and independent deities, generally father, mother and son ; but nowhere is it taught that God is one in three Hypostases.   In very early times we hear of a *Pawit* (*Paut*) or Company of the chief deities, consisting of nine gods and goddesses.   These were divided into three groups of three each, perhaps the best known being that of Osiris, his wife Isis, and their son the younger Horus.   At Heliopolis was the triad formed of Tum, Rā', and Harmakhis ; at Thebes by Amon, Mût and Khonsu.   At Heliopolis there was at first, however, a company of nine deities, four pairs of which emanated from Tum, the ancient Sun-god of that district.   The first of these emanations were Shu and Tefnut.   When these nine deities were formed into triads, Prof. Maspero tells us, the son of each divine couple was identified with Shu. This idea spread to other Egyptian triads.   Then Tum and Shu, father and son, were identified with each other, and so on in each group, the mother in each case being confounded with her husband and her child.   This is supposed to have led to a belief that each triad was really one and the same deity under a variety of names.   Thus, according to Maspero, in Egypt :

In comparatively early times the theologians were busy uniting in a single person the prerogatives which their ancestors had ascribed to many different beings.   But this conception of deity towards which their ideas were converging has nothing in common with the conception of the God of our modern religions and philosophies.   No god of the Egyptians was ever spoken of simply as " God."   Tum was " the one and only god " . . . at Heliopolis ; Anhuri-Shu was also " the one and only god " at Sebennytos and at Thinis.[1]   The unity of Tum did not interfere with that of Anhuri-Shu, but each of these gods, although the " sole " deity in his own domain, ceased to be so in the domain of the other.

---

[1] *Sic*, for *This*.

The feudal spirit, always alert and jealous, prevented the higher dogma, which was dimly apprehended in the temples, from triumphing over local religions and extending over the whole land. Egypt had as many " sole " deities as she had large cities, or even important temples ; she never accepted the idea of the sole God " beside whom there is none other." [1]

Hence we see what a vast difference there is between the ancient Egyptian belief in a large number of gods, divided into family groups of father, mother, and son, on the one hand, and the Christian doctrine of the Trinity on the other. Of course we know that *trias* is the Greek word for Trinity, and that certain modern scholars have in a loose way used the word " trinity " to express their idea about the Egyptian as well as the Hindû (and even certain Greek and Roman) groups of deities. But this does not alter the fact which has been stated. In Egypt we see a multitude of deities resolving itself into a limited number of triads, and the members of these triads becoming confounded with one another, until each triad approached absorption into a single god, thus leaving one god for each chief city or temple. In the Christian doctrine of the Trinity, on the other hand, we find an attempt to express in theological terms the distinct teaching of the New Testament on the subject of the Nature of God. To put the matter philosophically, the New Testament shows how the One God, belief in Whom was the inheritance of the Jewish Church, could be both Transcendent and Immanent, and had revealed Himself as Father, Son, and Holy Spirit. This is quite a different matter. Nor is there any room for doubt as to the origin of our belief in the Trinity. It was taught us by Christ and His Apostles, as a careful study of the New Testament shows.

III. Some people are said to solve the question of the

[1] Maspero, *The Dawn of Civilization*, pp. 151, 152.

relation in which Christianity stands to other religions in a very summary way, by saying, " Christianity is right and all the rest are wrong." In one sense, doubtless, this is true, but it is not the whole truth. Perhaps no *absolutely* false system of religion has ever prevailed among men. What makes any falsehood dangerous is the amount of truth which it contains. All religions contain some truth, as we have already seen. A false religion, therefore, is not one completely devoid of truth ; it is a faith in which truths are so perverted and mixed with error that the result is evil rather than good. Islâm offers an example of this. Its creed consists, as Gibbon has well said, of an eternal truth and a necessary fiction : " There is no god but God ; Muhammad is the Apostle of God." The first part of this creed teaches the purest Monotheism and commends itself to men everywhere as an eternal and necessary truth, when it is carefully considered : the second part of it has introduced all the evils, moral, social, political, religious, intellectual, under which Muslim countries have for centuries been groaning. Zoroastrianism, again, at least in its later form, taught that good would finally triumph over evil ; yet its doctrine of Dualism, i.e., its belief in two Creators, a good, Ôrmazd (Ahura-Mazdâ) and an evil, Ahriman (Añrô-Mainyuš), its laudation of incestuous marriages, and its polytheism, are among the things which stamp it as by no means a true faith. Christians gladly and thankfully welcome whatever truths they find in any religion, for our principle in these matters is that so well expressed by Augustine : " Whoever is a good and true Christian, let him recognize that truth, wherever he may have found it, belongs to his Lord," Who is Himself the Truth as well as the Way and the Life. It is right to cleanse the jewel of truth from the mire of error into which it has fallen in heathen religions, and not to condemn jewel and mire alike. Yet the modern " liberal " and " broad-minded " way of accepting both mire and jewel is hardly wise *or even cleanly*. The truth in all religions comes from God in some way : the error *does not*. It may seem " narrow-minded " to differentiate between the two, but it is none the less both the Christian and the common-sense way after all.

IV. Another view is that all religions alike are the result of evolution—that marvellous word which, many people fancy, explains everything, though itself under-stood by none.[1]   According to this theory, the superiority of Christianity to all other faiths is the natural result of its later development. It is the last of its series, and therefore the best. It has even been urged that there was actually being developed in the Græco-Roman world a system of ethics almost exactly similar to that taught by Christianity, only the latter was a little premature in its arrival and then crushed out the hopeful germ in the general overthrow of the heathen religions of the Empire. Now the evolutionary hypothesis [2] in regard to religion has its attractions, but unfortunately the facts are against it. The truth underlying it is doubtless that we can trace a gradual progress (in one family) in the Divine education [3] of the human race, but we cannot say that

[1] At least Herbert Spencer's explanation of it will help but few of us to understand it.   He defines Evolution as, " A change from an indefinite coherent heterogeneity to a definite coherent heterogeneity through continuous differentiations and integra-tions " (*Data of Ethics*, p. 65).

[2] More fully dealt with in ch. xvi., below.

[3] There was " education " being carried on elsewhere, in the *failure* of religions and philosophies to retain or attain a know-

Christianity sprang naturally either from the Pharisaism or the Sadduceeism or even the Essenism of the Jews, or from the Messianism of the Jewish Apocalyptic books. Still less can we trace it even in imagination to the Roman, Greek, Egyptian, Persian, Syrian, Babylonian systems of religion. These were steadily dying out, some were nearly dead when Christ came. Even in Egypt belief in an After-life was waxing faint, while in the Græco-Roman world proper universal despair and unbelief were the sad note of poets, historians, moralists and philosophers alike. As early as about 270 B.C. we find this feeling expressed by Moschus [1] in these lines :

> Alas, alas ! The mallows in the garden when they fade,
> Or parsley green and anise, blooming crisply in the glade,
> Though withered now, yet spring again and live another year ;
> But *we*, the great, the mighty, e'en the wisest, soon as here
> We once are dead, unhearing lie within the hollow ground,
> Sleeping a sleep unending, unawaking, drear, profound.

How full Catullus, Lucretius, and Horace are of the same hopelessness is well known. Coupled with it went, as it always does, the sentiment, " Let us eat and drink, for to-morrow we die." [2] So in Egypt also we find an inscription in the grave of a minor priest of Amon, Nefer-hotep, which may be thus freely rendered : " Enjoy the day, O priest, apply to thyself scented oil, fine oil, . . . thy sister, the delight of thine heart, sitting by thy side. Let the harper make music before thee. Put behind thee every ill. Recall joy to thyself ; for that day cometh on which thou must depart to the silence-loving land."

Despair was the prevalent note of dying heathenism,

---

ledge of God. Hence Plato learnt the need of some " Divine Word."

[1] Idyll, iii., *Lament for Bion*, vv. 99–106.

[2] Cf. *Horace :* Carpe diem, quam minime credula postero."

joy and faith that of nascent Christianity. The two were as opposite as the poles ; hence the centuries of bitter struggle, filled with torture, persecution, martyrdom, from which the Christian Church emerged victorious. In the same way, the Judaism of the time had either become half heathenized (as among the Herodians), or rationalized out of all spirituality (as among the Sadducees), or made into a hard and austere system of legalism (as among the Pharisees). The early history of the Church shows that the Jews were at least as hostile to the Church of Christ as were the Gentiles. Now it might be still conceivably possible that a new system of religion might somehow arise from Judaism or Hellenism, but it is not conceivable that such a system should in any real sense be evolved out of either, in the sense that either or both were earlier stages in the evolution of that new system. There was certainly a Divine *preparation* for Christianity going on in the Gentile world as well as in the Jewish, even if we do not go so far as to say with some of the early Christian writers, that philosophy in the Græco-Roman world played much the same part in that preparation as did the Law in the Jewish. But preparation and evolution are very different things.

As for ethics, it is doubtless true that one can compile many excellent moral precepts from the Greek and Latin poets and philosophers, just as we can from the Persian literature of the present day. But the expression of noble ideas, which no one ever practises or has any motive power to make him even desirous of practising, is worth very little. Socrates and Epictetus seem, as far as we know, to have been the only preachers of ethics in the heathen world who really strove to live up to what they taught ; and what very lax notions of sexual morality, for instance, Socrates himself entertained it is easy to learn from the writings of his disciples, Plato and Xenophon. Most of the moralists of the time, like Seneca, might well have expressed the truth about themselves by saying with Ovid :

> " What is good I perceive, and I praise it ;
>   But the evil I do."

So far was the heathen world from evolving a noble system of morality for itself that it rejected the ethics of Christianity when offered to it, and perished of its own incurable vices.[1]

Historically, too, we know that Christianity is not a mere ethical system. *Christianity is Christ.* No one can honestly say that he believes that Christ's character, even if regarded as ideal and imaginary, was evolved out of Judaism or from the heathenism of the first century of our era. That it was not an imaginary but a real[2] character is as clear as anything in human history can possibly be. An unbeliever says : " It must be admitted that there are few characters of antiquity about whom we possess so much indubitably historical information."[3]   A very thoughtful writer of our own time puts the matter thus :[4] " The one thing that seems to defy the solvents of Rationalism is the Personality of Christ. . . . Nothing can take away the wonder and sublimity of His teaching and of His example. We may ransack the records of humanity in vain for such a figure, such a

[1] Sencovich's *Quo Vadis* gives a good idea of the state of society under Nero.
[2] Vide *Religio Critici*, ch. ii., " The Fact of Christ."
[3] Schweitzer's *Quest of the Historical Jesus*, p. 6.
[4] A. C. Benson, *The Gate of Death*.

life, such a conception of moral virtue." It would be easy to multiply examples of such testimony as this.

The contrast between Christianity and the highest imaginings of the Græco-Roman world could hardly be more clearly set forth than in the following passage from Mr. Lecky [1] :

The Platonist exhorted men to imitate God ; the Stoic, to follow reason ; the Christian, to the love of Christ. The later Stoics had often united their notions of excellence in an ideal sage, and Epictetus had even urged his disciples to set before them some man of surpassing excellence, and to imagine him continually near them ; but the utmost the Stoic ideal could become was a model for imitation, and the admiration it inspired could never deepen into affection. It was reserved for Christianity to present to the world an ideal character, which, through all the changes of eighteen centuries, has inspired the hearts of men with an impassioned love, has shown itself capable of acting on all ages, nations, temperaments, and conditions, has been not only the highest pattern of virtue but the strongest incentive to its practice, and has exercised so deep an influence that it may be truly said that the simple record of three short years of active life has done more to regenerate and to soften mankind than all the disquisitions of philosophers and all the exhortations of moralists. This has, indeed, been the wellspring of whatever is best and purest in the Christian life. Amid all the sins and failings, amid all the priestcraft and persecution and fanaticism that have defaced the Church, it has preserved, in the character and example of its Founder, an enduring principle of regeneration.

As more than nineteen hundred years have elapsed since Christ's birth, and as, even with His example to imitate, humanity has never yet produced any other character in the remotest degree worthy to be brought into comparison with Him, there must be something very wrong in the theory that Christianity is the result of the evolutionary process. Here, again, facts confute the

[1] *History of Morals*, vol. ii., p. 9.

theory : but, were it true, Christianity would even then be the Absolute Religion.

V. Only one other view need here be considered, viz., that Christianity is the self-revelation of God in Christ, the final lesson in the religious education of the human race. Its true relation to other religions has been well expressed in these words : " The pre-Christian religions were the age-long prayer : the Incarnation was the answer." [1] The truth of this view is proved by all history, including that of philosophy, and by all human experience. Christ has shown Himself to be the fulfilment of the highest hopes, the deepest needs, the unconscious prophecies of heathendom, and of men's noblest guesses at truth. Whether we take the Messianic prophecies of Judaism as pious hopes, as faint foreshadowings, or as Divine promises, they, too, have found their fulfilment in Him. He is the Head of the human race, and at the same time the only character [2] from Which we men of the twentieth century can form a worthy conception of the Invisible God. As a plain matter of fact, apart from all theological dogmas, in Him and in Him alone God and man meet. Hence it is that those who reject Him are compelled for the most part to reject God, or at least to acknowledge their ignorance of Him and their inability to know Him. Even on this supposition, all the religious yearnings of the race and its instinct of worship would be meaningless and unaccountable, a fact which of itself proves that Agnosticism cannot be justified. But a lower level still remains, and that is reached in a recent book [3] which declares that a belief in God seems

[1] Illingworth in *Lux Mundi*, p. 208.
[2] Vide *Religio Critici*, ch. i., *initio*.
[3] Leuba, *Psychological Origin and Nature of Religion, fin.*

no longer possible, and that man therefore needs an efficient, impersonal substitute.

Since, therefore, in our own day the choice lies between God as revealed in Christ and no God at all ; since the former position explains the universal religious instinct of humanity, shows its adequate object, and satisfies man's spiritual yearnings for the Living God, while the latter fails to account for that which has in all ages exercised the very mightiest of all influences on the whole human race, and confesses its inability to solve the problem not only of the existence of religion, but of the existence of the universe itself ; it follows that the successful solution is to be preferred to the unsuccessful. It thus becomes clear what is the relation in which Christianity stands to all other religions, and how well justified is its claim to be the Absolute and the Universal faith, being the last stage in the religious education of the race, God's final revelation of Himself to man.

CHAPTER V

God's Nature and Attributes according to Christianity and other Religions

IT is a matter of the utmost difficulty, in the first place, to conceive in one's own mind the religious sentiments of men of other faiths than our own; and, in the second, to express these ideas in such a way as not to mislead one's readers. Even at the present day such words as *God, Paradise, Salvation, twice-born, union with God,* convey to a Christian ideas entirely different from those which a Hindû receives from them. " Twice-born " (*dvi-ja*) to a Hindû means " belonging to one of the three primary castes," while " union (*yoga*) with God " means loss of personality and absorption into the impersonal It (*tat*) which alone exists. The word which in Latin has now come [1] to mean " God " (*Deus*) in its Hindî form *deo* and its Persian form *dîv* means rather a demon. If such difficulty exists in expressing the religious ideas of men of our own time, and of the same Âryan stock, in such a manner as to make them intelligible to our readers and to avoid misleading them utterly,

---

[1] In Greek the meaning of θεός was elevated (1) by the writings of the philosophers, and (2) by the translation of the Old Testament into Greek (the Septuagint Version). Then Greek philosophy introduced a higher significance into the Latin *Deus.*

it may easily be understood that it is still more difficult
to represent at all correctly the mental and religious
attitude of men of the past.   To give a literal translation
of a passage from the *Rig-Veda,* or the Book of the Dead,
for instance, is easy : but when every single theological
term there employed conveys to us an idea almost absolutely different from that which the original readers of
such books understood by it, the most accurate rendering is apt to prove the most misleading.   Christianity
has raised all such terms, purified them, and invested
them with such a wealth of beauty and significance
that we are almost compelled to read into the books of
other religions lofty Christian conceptions which certainly never occurred to the minds of the heathen of
old, nor do so now to the present representatives of these
ancient faiths, if (like Hindûism and Buddhism) they
still maintain an independent existence.

The Egyptians, for instance, in common with not a
few other ancient peoples, conceived of their gods as
corporeal, possessing bodies as material as their own.
An old inscription [1] speaks of the Sun-god Rā' as having
his flesh of silver, his hair of gold, his sinews of genuine
lapis-lazuli.   This was the belief of the Egyptians of
historical times.   So also Osiris is said to have been
slain [2] and his *body* to have been cut in pieces and scattered
far and wide by Set.   It was collected by his sister-
wife, Isis, mummified and buried, some said in one place
in Egypt, some in another ; and it was believed to
remain buried there, just as the bodies of ordinary
Egyptians lay embalmed in their tombs.   The pre-historic
inhabitants of the country worshipped various animals
as gods, such as the lion, the hawk, the serpent, the

[1] In the tomb of Seti I.   [2] See our concluding chapter.

E

ibis ; and this form of religion continued, along with the higher, as long as the nation itself. Belief in such material deities, often bestial, is hard for us to conceive of as possible : hence attempts have been made to explain these as merely representations of certain Divine attributes ; but the evidence to the contrary is too strong to be resisted. It is well to remember the *materiality* of the deities worshipped even now by many different tribes in various parts of the world, and to keep in mind the fact that in Babylonia, Assyria, Greece and other lands the same idea prevailed in heathen times, even though some few philosophers may occasionally have entertained loftier conceptions.

In reference to the Nature of God it is possible to trace historically whatever advance has been made from early days to the present. It should never be forgotten, however, that there is good reason to believe that in times still more remote, before the rise of polytheism, more worthy conceptions of the Divine prevailed. Traces of these may be occasionally detected in the most ancient written records which have come down to us in different countries. What is said about Varuṇa in the *Rig-Veda*, for example, discloses a higher idea of the Divine than anything found in ordinary Hindûism to-day. But these lofty ideas were gradually lost, partly through men's desire to have gods of like passions with themselves, and partly (it may be) through the influence of a form of primitive philosophy, largely materialistic. At any rate, in many faiths there meets us a kind of evolutionary view of the origin of all things from primeval matter. This is a very remarkable fact in the history of human thought. We proceed to adduce a few instances in support of this statement.

One of the earliest Babylonian myths relative to the coming into existence of all things begins thus [1] :—

When the heavens above had not proclaimed
(And) the earth below had not mentioned a name,
Then the Abyss [*apsu*] was their begetter,
The Water of the Deep (or *Mummu Ti'âmtim*) was the genetrix
    of them all.
Their waters also were united into one.
A field was not yet marked out, marsh was not yet seen,
When the gods had appeared not, not one.
A name they mentioned not, destiny they had not fixed.
Then the gods Kiš[ar and Anšar [2]] were made,
The god Laḥmu and the goddess Laḥamu appeared.

Here we see belief that all things, even the gods, sprang from original matter, and that this matter, divided into two parts, produced the gods by a generative process. The idea of creation is here laid aside in favour of what is correctly termed cosmogony, " the *generation* of the world." From very early times most nations have been obsessed with the idea that *progenitiveness* was the golden key to unlock the mystery of existence. We cannot continue to deal with such an unsavoury subject, but its influence on the history of almost all heathen religions has been enormous, and perhaps in every case it has produced the vilest possible results.

The materialistic philosophy underlying this myth shows itself in the last line quoted above, as well as in the mention of the Abyss and the Waters of the Deep. It is not quite certain what Laḥmu and Laḥamu mean, but they seem connected with a word which in Hebrew and Aramaic means *bread*, while in Arabic it means

---

Cuneiform Texts from Babylonian Tablets in the British Museum, Pt. xiii., plate 1, lines 1-10.
[2] I.e., " the hosts of earth and of heaven."

flesh. Perhaps, therefore, " the god Laḥmu and the goddess Laḥamu " signify two forms of matter, masculine and feminine. The analogy of other systems confirms this theory, as we shall see.

Another account,[1] fragmentary at the beginning, tells us how creation proper began—apparently after the emergence of the gods from matter. It says :—

" The whole of the lands was sea, at the time that within the sea there was a waterspring." It goes on to state that the god Ea, " King of the Bright Mound," founded his house in the midst of the Abyss (*apsu*), and afterwards made the gods and the Earth-spirits (*Anunnaki*). Then Bel[2] Merodach " bound a raft on the face of the water : he made dust and poured it out with the sea. He brought the gods into the seat of the good of his heart " (i.e., the place of which he approved). " He made mankind. The goddess Aruru " (Beltu, " the lady," Bel's wife) " the seed of mankind with him made,"

Turning to Egypt, we find on the walls of the pyramid of Pepi I. a passage very similar to the first of the two which we have quoted above. There, speaking of the time before the beginning of the world, it is written :—

At that time the heaven was not, the earth was not, men did not exist, the gods were not born, there was no death.[3]

But Professor Sayce thinks that this is merely a survival of the Babylonian myth, brought in very early times from Babylonia by the dynastic Egyptians, who

[1] Op. cit., plate 35, lines 10, *sqq.* We have the text in both Sumerian and Assyrian.

[2] Otherwise En Lil.

[3] Quoted by Sayce, *Religions of Ancient Egypt and Babylonia,* 1st ed., p. 238.

conquered the more ancient inhabitants of the valley of the Nile.

The genuine original Egyptian belief, however, seems to have been somewhat similar.   From Nû, the primeval deep, and Nût, the sky, all things apparently sprang. Sib, the Earth-god, symbolized by a goose, laid the mundane egg from which came the universe.   Sib was the father of Osiris.   Nû and another Nût became parents of three groups of beings, each consisting of a male and a female principle, named Ḥeḥui and Ḥeḥet (*eternity*), Kek and Keket (*darkness*), and Nini and Ninit (*inertia?*). The " company of the gods " are sprung from *Paut*, a word which Erman renders by Antiquity (*Urzeit*), but which, there is good reason to believe, more probably means " matter," as in ordinary use it denoted " cake," " food," thus reminding us of the *Laḥmu* and *Laḥamu* of Babylonia.   The Egyptian word for a god, *nuter*, *nuther*, comes from a root meaning " to spring up, to grow like a plant."   Hence, at least in later times, Rā' and other gods are said to have come into existence by themselves (*Kheper t'es-ef*), which term is also used of plants and certain mineral formations.[1]   This again reminds us of an address of Sennacherib to Asshur, the chief deity of Assyria.   It runs thus [2] :—

To Asshur, King of the Company of the Gods, *maker of himself*
    (*bânû ramnišu*) father of the gods,
Whose form grew in the Abyss, King of heaven and earth,
Lord of all gods, moulder of the Heavenly spirits (*Igigi*) and of
    the Earth-spirits (*Anunnaki*),

---

[1] Does this show that the modern idea that crystallization and cell-growth are akin occurred to the ancients, as did the atomic theory ?

[2] Brit. Mus. " K.," 5413, A. ; vide F. Martin's *Textes Religi eux assyriens et babyloniens*, Pt. i., p. 312.

Former of the heaven of Anu and the lower earth, maker of al l
    men,
Inhabiter of the bright blue sky, lord of the gods, fixer of fates,
    etc.

If we turn to Ancient China, something not quite
unlike the Babylonian and Egyptian belief meets us.

[1] Before the beginning of all things there was Nothing. In the
lapse of ages, Nothing coalesced into Unity, the Great Monad.
After more ages, the Great Monad [2] separated into duality, the
male and female principles in Nature : and then, by a process of
biogenesis, the visible universe was produced. Popular cosmogony goes on to say that the male and female principles were
each subdivided into Greater and Lesser ; and then, from the
interaction of these four agencies, a being named P'ân Ku came
into existence. He . . . is often depicted as wielding a huge
adze and engaged in constructing the world. With his death the
details of existence began. His breath became the wind ; his
voice the thunder ; his left eye the sun ; his right eye the moon ;
his blood flowed in rivers ; his hair grew into trees and plants ;
his flesh became the soil ; his sweat descended as rain ; while
the parasites which infested his body were the origin of the human
race.[3]

Here all mention of God and creation are lacking.
Yet the Chinese had two terms for God, both of which
occur in documents which go back to about 2,000 B.C.
One of these is Shang-ti, " the Supreme Ruler " ; the
other T'ien, " Heaven." The former, however, has
come to include the spirits of dead Emperors of China,
and the latter the material sky. Unfortunately, so little
is said of the Deity in the oldest Chinese literature that it
is difficult to know what conception of the Divine was

[1] Prof. Giles, *Religions of Ancient China*, pp. 7, 8.
[2] This bears a curious resemblance to later Pythagorean
philosophy.
[3] Almost exactly the same idea occurs in Scandinavian mythology regarding the giant Ymir, and in Indian about Purusha,
slain by the gods. *Vide* p. 220.

then entertained. Confucius himself " did much towards weakening the personality of God, for whom he invariably used T‘ien, never Shang-ti, regarding Him evidently more as an abstraction than as a living, sentient Being, with the physical attributes of a man."[1]   He tells us, however, that " by their great sacrificial ceremonies the ancients served God," though he adds, " by their ceremonies in the ancestral temple they worshipped their forefathers."[2]   Ancestor-worship was even then, therefore, taking the place of the worship of God, as we have already seen.

Even in Confucius' time,[3] and long before it, the philosophic system known as Taouism had become the general faith of China.   It represents, no doubt, a degeneration of earlier ideas, but has to be considered in tracing our present subject historically.   *Tao* or *Taou* means " Path " or " Way," as denoting " the way, course or movement of the Universe, her processes and methods."[4]   Taouism " conceives the Universe as one large organism of powers and influences, a living machine, the core of which is the Great Ultimate Principle, or *T‘ai Kih*, comprising the two cosmic Breaths or Souls, known as the Yang and the Yin, of which respectively Heaven and Earth are the chief depositories.   These two Souls produce the four seasons and the phenomena of Nature. . . .   It is they also that produce and animate the five elements, which are the constituents of the material and immaterial world. . . .   The Universe is filled up in all its parts with *shen* or *yang* spirits, which

[1] Giles, op. cit., pp. 36, 37.
[2] Op. cit., p. 30.
[3] B.C. 551–478.
[4] De Groot, *The Religious System of China*, vol. i., pp. 66–68.

animate everything that exists, and regulate the Tao of Nature and its phenomena or revolutions."

It was probably because of this Animism which had gradually usurped the place of belief in God (Shang-ti, the " Supreme Lord "), that such Agnostic philosophies as those of Confucius, Mencius, and Laou-tsze,[1] arose in China, to give men something which seemed more in accordance with reason. Much the same process, with a similar result, has followed in other countries also. In Laou-tsze's philosophy no personal God is recognized : yet his followers now worship Laou-tsze himself as " the three Pure Ones," meaning apparently the three images representing Past, Present, and Future, which are adored as in some way recalling him. They have, however, invented a deity styled " the Precious, Imperial God," in connexion with whom they worship the stars (especially Jupiter, Mercury, Mars, and Saturn, and also the Great Bear), mountains, rivers, valleys, the God of Thunder, the Mother of Lightning, the Spirit of the Sea, the Dragon King (whose manifestations are snakes) and many other deities. They have fallen into degraded idolatry, mixed with charlatanry and vice.[2]

We now turn to Ancient India in order to see what conception of the Divine existed among the Âryans of that land. The Drâvidians of early days have left us no records by which to judge of their ideas on the subject. But the views of the Âryans are of especial interest to us, because they reveal what must have been, in some measure at least, the thoughts of our own Âryan fore-fathers too, as well as those of the early Greeks, Romans, Persians and Slavonians, before their literature arose.

[1] The founder of Taouism as a school of philosophy.
[2] Sir R. K. Douglas, *Confucianism and Taouism*, pp. 211–287.

In Vedic India there were at least thirty-three gods
adored, besides minor deities. The religion actually
current was a system of Nature-worship. The sun,
moon, stars, earth, sky, rivers, mountains, the wind,
the gods of the atmosphere and the storm, and many
others, including fire and the intoxicating juice of the
Soma-plant, were personified, and received divine honours.
Hymns, prayers and sacrifices were offered to them.
There were, however, two great classes of deities, the
Asuras and the Devas, of whom the former were adored
by the latter in early times. All the gods were the
offspring of Dyaus, the god of the bright sky (corresponding to the Greek Zeus and the Latin Jove) and of Aditi
(" the Expanse," often identified with Pṛithivî, the Earth),
just as in Greece the deities sprang from Heaven (*Ouranos*)
and Earth (*Gaia*).[1] The seven Âdityas or sons of Aditi
were not all of equal importance, the chief among them
being Varuṇa, Mitra and Aryaman. The attributes of
Varuṇa in the Vedic Hymns [2] are such as to lead to the
belief that in him we may find the survival of a purer
faith than Nature-worship. His robe is the sky, his
breath the storm, and the sun is his eye. He has established earth and sky on unshakeable foundations, fixed
the stars in the firmament, and marked out the paths
of the streams. He is the maker and preserver of all
things, knows present, past, and future, and views everything from his palace with a thousand gates in the highest
heaven. He has laid down moral laws, and he watches
over their execution with unsleeping eye. Yet, as has
been said, in the Vedas he is but one of many gods.

---

[1] Hesiod, *Theogonia*, vv. 126–137. But Zeus was also " father
of gods and men."

[2] Cf. especially *Rig-Veda*, iv., 42 ; vii., 80, 88, 89 ; x., 14.

In the later Hymns of the *Rig-Veda* we find the Pantheism which has ever since pervaded Indian thought. It doubtless arose from philosophy such as was more fully developed in the Upanishads. The earliest Hymn which deals with the cosmogony runs thus [1]:—

1. When the Non-existent was not, and the Existent was not, then the Atmosphere was not and Heaven above was not. What also existed below ? Where, in whose treasury, was the water ? What was the deep abyss ?

2. Then Death was not, Deathlessness was not, Light of Night, of Day, was not : that One Thing breathed breathless of itself ; nothing else was there beside it, whatever [since] has been.

3. At first there was Darkness enveloped in darkness [2] ; un-illumined was all this flood. When the Emptiness was concealed by the Void, then with might the One Thing was born from Heat. . . .

6. Who knows for certain, who would here explain ? Whence, whence did this Product [the world] originate ? *The gods were later than its production*, then who knows whence it sprang ?

7. Whence this Product sprang, whether it was created or not, He who is its overseer in the highest heaven, He only knows—or even He knows not.

A less poetic but hardly more philosophic cosmogony is given in the Chhândogya Upanishad (Book VI., ch. ii. 1–3) [3] :—

In the beginning there was that thing only which is, one only, without a second (*Ekam evâdvitîyam*). Others say, In the beginning there was that only which is not, one only without a second ; and from that which is not that which is was born. . . . Only that which is was in the beginning, one only without a second. It thought, " Let me be many, let me grow out." It sent forth

---

[1] *Rig-Veda*, x., 129.

[2] This resembles the chaos which Hesiod represents as the first thing to come into existence : *Theog.* 116–118.

[3] To prevent misunderstanding, I use *ch* to represent the letter thus pronounced but usually transliterated by *c* in Sanskrit, and therefore *chh* instead of the letter for which the more common transliteration is now *ch*.

fire (*tejas*). That fire thought, " Let me be many, let me grow out." It sent forth water. And, therefore, whenever any one is hot anywhere and perspires, water is produced upon him from fire alone. Water thought, " Let me be many, let me grow out." It sent forth earth [literally " food," *anna* : cf. what has been said above about the Babylonian *Laḥmu* and the Egyptian *Paut*].

The *Hiraṇyagarbha* (" Golden Germ ") is in one of the Hymns of the *Rig-Veda* mentioned as that from which the universe came into existence.[1] This idea recurs in many parts of the world. The gods sprang from original matter accordingly. The progeneration idea is found very fully established in early Hindûism, as in so many other Nature-religions. One myth states that the deity felt not delight, being alone. He wished for a companion, and therefore divided his own body into two parts, husband and wife. Thus human beings were brought into existence.[2]

It is hardly necessary to do more than to remind our readers how closely akin Greek ideas on these subjects were to those of the Hindûs. But it may be of interest to quote the traditions of a people very far removed from Babylonians, Egyptians, Chinese, Hindûs and Greeks in culture and race—the Polynesians. The Maori tradition states that at first the world existed in darkness. Its two parts, Heaven and Earth (Rangi and Papa) were united and formed a globe, in the centre of which lay the gods.[3] At the instigation of one of

[1] In Manu's *Dharmaśâstra*, Bk. I., *initio*, it is said that when the " self-existent " (*svayambhu*, cf. what has been said about the same term in Babylonian and Egyptian religion) Brahman produced the waters, he placed a seed therein. This seed grew into a golden germ or egg, shining like the sun, and from it came forth the Creator Brahmâ.

[2] *Śatapatha Brâhmaṇa*, XIV., iv., 2, 1.

[3] There is a remarkable likeness between what the Pyramid

their number, they all with one exception agreed to separate the sky from the earth, so that light might enter and man be made. By a sudden effort the god who proposed the scheme raised the sky aloft by standing on his head and striking upward with his feet.

Nobler ideas of the deities, however, were found in other sections of the Polynesian race. In nearly all of them a god called Tangaroa was worshipped. The Samoans held that he was born of the " Cloudless Heaven " and of the " Expanded Heaven," very much as, among the Hindûs, Varuṇa was son of Dyaus and Aditi. Originally existing in space, Tangaroa created the Heavens for his dwelling place, and afterwards he made the earth. The people of Tahiti said that, when as yet " there was no sea, no earth, no heaven, no human beings," he lived in space. He was Father of gods and men : he was called the Root, the Rock, the Light.

This is an example of the fact that unlettered and almost savage tribes have often retained a loftier and more spiritual idea of the Divine than highly civilized nations. In *The Making of Religion*, Mr. A. Lang proves most clearly that belief in a Good Spirit, often considered as ready to answer prayer, as never having died, as needing no sacrifices (in the way of food), as do the inferior deities, and as having created the world, is to be found among even the lowest savages in Patagonia, Australia, Greenland, the Andaman Islands, Melanesia, British Guiana, and in many other places. Among barbarians in a more advanced state such belief is often much fainter, instead of being clearer and nobler. It existed, however, pretty generally among the North

Texts say of one god eating the others and the Maori legend to the same effect.

American Indians, and traces of it were found in ancient Peru, where a high degree of material civilization had lowered and degraded religious conceptions. The reason of the latter fact is doubtless that, as civilization and its attendant luxury and worldliness have always (unless in some measure counteracted by Christianity in later times) led men to indulge in shameful vices, from which even savages are comparatively free, in lowering their moral tone it has lowered their conceptions of the Divine, and sometimes almost entirely obliterated them. Men are very apt to create their gods in their own image. Hume [1] has well said, " There is an universal tendency among mankind to conceive all beings like themselves, and to transfer to every object those qualities with which they are familiarly acquainted, and of which they are intimately conscious. . . . Nor is it long before we ascribe to them thought and reason and passion, and sometimes even the limbs and figures of men, in order to bring them nearer to a resemblance with ourselves." Thus the tales of Zeus and Ganymede, Kṛishṇa and the Gopîs, Ishtar and her many lovers, throw a terrible light on the character of the people that worshipped such deities.

Much that we now know of the religious ideas of the Gentile world is so unspeakably vile that we cannot defile our pages by dwelling upon it. Classical readers will remember what Herodotus says of the worship of Mylitta at Babylon, and what Lucian, Strabo and many other writers tell us about much the same kind of service of the gods and goddesses in other parts of Asia. The same thing prevailed in Canaan before the Hebrew conquest, and reasserted itself before the Babylonian

[1] *Natural History of Religion*, Sect. II.

captivity. In Egypt the Pyramid Texts indicate something similar in connexion with Isis-worship and that of Osiris, and in India the same thing is practised to the present day. Phallic worship was one of the most popular forms which Physiolatry (the worship of the powers of Nature) assumed almost throughout the world. The reproductive power of Nature appealed to men as the greatest of all mysteries and as the highest of the Divine attributes. This heathen view is expressed and defended, and its natural influence in encouraging immorality shown all too sympathetically, by a modern French writer,[1] in these words : " That sacred fire, which suddenly kindles the blood, and lifts two mortals from earth to heaven ; for it is to approach the Divinity, to give oneself up with religious fervour to the most noble and irresistible sentiment that He has implanted within us, the only sentiment that, in His adorable wisdom, the Dispenser of all good has vouchsafed to sanctify, by endowing it with a spark of His own creative energy." Unpleasant as it is to refer to this matter, it is impossible to give any true account of the prevailing conception of the Divine among almost all the civilized nations of antiquity without indicating a view at once the most widespread, the most influential, and the most degrading of all. It will now be realized, at least in some measure, how completely all idea of a *Holy* God had from a very early time been banished from the minds of all the leading and cultured peoples and of many of the less prominent tribes in the ancient world.

All this corruption of religion and perversion of the religious sentiment led to a second stage in the

---

[1] Eugene Sue, *The Wandering Jew*, Pt. III., cap. xli.

history of Gentile religious thought. We must now proceed to inquire what this was.

Among many people, alike among the thoughtful and the unthinking, this degradation of religion led to Atheism. Men could not believe in such gods and goddesses as were depicted in classical poetry, Greek, Sanskrit, or other. Hence many ridiculed the very idea of the existence of any gods at all, feeling that no religion was better than such a religion as they had inherited. Others, more earnest and thoughtful, determined to discover through philosophy what their religion could not teach. Hence in India we find first the Upanishads, and then the Six " Orthodox " and the two great " Unorthodox " systems of philosophy. Some of these are Agnostic, others Atheistic. Where anything like belief in a Deity occurs, what is taught is Pantheism in one of its many varied forms. We have already seen that even in the later Hymns of the *Rig-Veda* evidences of this appear. Hence the philosophic basis of all Modern Hindûism is Pantheistic. It has indeed been said that Pantheism " rocked the cradle of Hindû religious thought." All the various deities were resolved into one, as were all other existent things. Hence the doctrine of the Chhândogya Upanishad, " There is only one Existent thing, without a second." Thus a Unity was conceived of, which might be styled the Deity, " Brahman," though it was regarded as impersonal and unconscious, the " Existent Non-Existent " (*sadâsat*).

Pantheism seems to have a tendency to recur whenever religion has reached a low stage, or whenever men reject revelation. It asserts itself in the Jewish Zôhar, and in Spinoza. Even in Sir Oliver Lodge's recent speculations on "Man and the Universe" we find the same tendency : in his case because he has not yet come to acknowledge in its fullest sense the essential Deity of the Lord Jesus Christ. Owing to the same cause Pantheism is undoubtedly spreading among us western Âryans, as long ago it began to spread among those of the east, and not among Âryans alone.

But alike in east and west, among the ancients as well as among the moderns, one of the many insuperable obstacles to accepting such a system instead of belief in a Personal God is that Pantheism deifies all the *evil* in the universe as well as all the good, and thus is absolutely immoral. If it is logical, it denies the existence of any real difference between right and wrong. This it has done in Hindûism. Sir Oliver Lodge completely fails to overcome this difficulty, and no wonder. Conscience cannot be explained in accordance with it, except as a huge mistake,[1] a delusion worthy of a lunatic. Nor can the Pantheistic conception of the Divine satisfy man's spiritual need of a Personal God. Nor again can such a theory be held to be in accordance with reason ; for it not only leaves unexplained the religious faculty in man, but also suffers shipwreck on the fact that the stream cannot by natural means rise higher than its source. As man possesses consciousness, personality, and a moral sense, the Source from which man sprang cannot be *lower* than man in these respects. The Divine Being must therefore be *at least* as fully conscious, personal, and moral, as is man, though these qualities may in Him reach a height as much superior to what we call

---

[1] How different this is from Kant's view of the Moral Law within !

personality,. etc., as personality is to the condition of a mineral. Even Herbert Spencer grants this.

Ancient Buddhism was Agnostic : modern Buddhism in many of its developments is Polytheistic. Yet the philosophic basis of the Mahâyâna Buddhism, as prevalent especially in China and Japan, is Pantheism, though it differs from much of Indian Pantheism in admitting the existence of certain of the higher attributes in the Deity. Thus a modern adherent of the system, speaking of this abstract Deity under the title of " the *Dharmakâya*," writes thus [1] :—

The Dharmakâya (which literally means " body, or system of being ") is, according to the Mahâyânists, the ultimate reality that underlies all particular phenomena ; it is that which makes the existence of individuals possible ; it is the *raison d'être* of the Universe ; it is the norm of Being, which regulates the course of events and thoughts. . . . The Dharmakâya may be compared in one sense to the " God " of Christianity, and in another sense to the " *brahman* " or " Paramâtman " of Vedântism. It is different, however, from the former in that it does not stand transcendentally above the Universe, which, according to the Christian view, was created by God, but which is, according to Mahâyânism, a manifestation of the Dharmakâya himself. It is also different from *brahman* in that it is not absolutely impersonal, nor is it a mere being. The Dharmakâya, on the contrary, is capable of willing and reflecting, or, to use Buddhist phraseology, it is *karuṇâ* (love) [2] and *bodhi* (intelligence), and not the mere state of being. This Pantheistic and at the same time *Entheistic* [3] Dharmakâya is working in every sentient being, for sentient beings are nothing but a self-manifestation of the Dharmakâya.

Elsewhere Suzuki adds, " All sentient beings, the Buddh a notexcepted, are one in the Dharmakâya." [4] He says that the Dharmakâya is " the Absolute or

---

[1] Suzuki, *Outlines of Mahâyâna Buddhism*, pp. 46, 47.

[2] *Karuṇâ* does not strictly mean " love," but rather " pity."

[3] Here apparently meaning *immanent*.

[4] Op. cit., p. 290.

F

Essence-body of all things,"[1] and admits that the teaching of Buddhism is that "there is no such thing as Ego-soul."[2]

Buddhism at its highest, therefore, entirely fails to find the Living God. The best it can offer is a declaration that the Universe is in some sort God, that man has no true personality, that he, the venomous reptile, evil and good spirits, all sentient things good and bad, are equally parts of a kind of Soul or Mind of the World (*Anima* or rather *Animus Mundi*), and that the world is itself alive and conscious.

The same causes produced much the same effect among the ancient Greek philosophers. Thales of Miletus (B.C. 600–550), who held that water was the source or origin of all things, taught that the universe was a living being, because of its continual motion. Anaximander (B.C. 610–547) believed that all things sprang from the infinite ($\tau\grave{o}$ $\mathring{a}\pi\epsilon\iota\rho o\nu$), by which he meant indeterminate matter, and ultimately returned to it again. This Infinite he held to be divine, and to contain and regulate all things. Anaximenes regarded the Universe as a living being, surrounded by air upon which it fed. He called the Universe, or rather the air from which it sprang, "God." Heraclitus believed that God was the soul of the Universe. All these four philosophers belonged to the Ionic School, and all recognized a great unity underlying the Universe : but they thought that this was unity of material, all things being formed out of one "element," though they differed as to what that "element" might be. They held much the same view of the Divine as is expressed in Pope's lines :—

---

[1] Op. cit., Introduction, p. 21.   [2] Op. cit., p. 38.

All are but parts of one stupendous whole,
Whose body Nature is, and God the soul.

Xenophanes of the Italic School (B.C. 520) held that "All is one." Disgusted at the vile tales told of the gods, he turned to philosophy, and declared that God was one only, but that He was an enormous sphere, unchanging, though conscious. However, this philosopher admitted his Agnosticism by stating that men could not attain to any true knowledge, but only to probability. Anaxagoras (B.C. 500) thought that Mind (νοῦς) brought order out of chaos. Mind is the soul of the Universe and is the principle of life in both animals and plants.

Plato reached much higher ground. He speaks of Mind as King of heaven and earth, believing that the Universe is a body animated by a Mind or Soul, which is God. This Deity bears the same relation to the Universe as does man's soul to his body, and possesses consciousness, reason, will. Man's soul is derived from that of the Universe, which is God, and is thus akin to this God, who is eternally existent in the future, though not in the past. For this God, incorporated in the Universe, was *created* together with the Universe by One higher God, Whom Plato in the *Timaeus* styles "the Creator," and Who existed from eternity. Matter, however, seems also to have been eternal. But though Plato had thus reached the great truth of the existence of One Eternal Creator and Father of the Universe, he makes hardly any use of it except as a theory. He says that it is a difficult task to discover Him, and impossible to speak of Him to all men. Hence to Plato also God was unknown, except in name.

Aristotle's language is vague regarding the nature of

the Deity. It sometimes approaches Deism, but is more frequently Pantheistic. He at one time seems to recognize design in the world, and at another declares that there is no Designer. There is a Supreme Mind giving commands to His armies, but this Mind is not the Architect of the Universe, it is rather the principle underlying it. It has energy but no volition, is eternal and self-existent like the Universe, it pervades the Universe and cannot be separated therefrom, it is both personal and impersonal. Absorbed in self-contemplation it is happy, but cares nothing for men's good deeds and bad. Aristotle, in fact, lost Plato's Primary God, and knew only the Secondary.

The Stoics recognized a Mind as governing the Universe as the soul the body, possessed of reason and consciousness. Him they sometimes called God, and even Creator. But yet they taught mere Pantheism, for they held that God is both matter and the energy which gives form to all that is made out of it. The visible Universe is a manifestation of Him and proceeds from Him. When destroyed, it will return to Him and eternally proceed forth again, cycle by cycle.[1]   Yet Stoics, such as Cleanthes (B.C. 300) whose noble Hymn to Zeus is well known, and who uses almost the same words as does Aratos, from whose " Phaenomena " (B.C. 270) St. Paul in Acts xvii. 28, quotes the words, " For His very offspring are we," were led by the " human soul, naturally Christian," within them to speak more fittingly of God than was quite in accordance with their philosophic creed. Believing in stern and unchangeable fate, they yet could pray to God, to Whom they gave the old Greek

[1] This reminds us of the Hindû doctrine of the *Kalpas* and of Brahmâ's alternate sleeping and waking.

name of Zeus. Evil and good might both be inherent
in the nature of things, yet, in spite of their philosophy,
they had a stern moral code, and called on men to strive
against the evil in themselves and pursue the good. In
not a few Stoics, and not least in the lame slave Epictetus
and the Emperor Marcus Aurelius, God "left not Himself without a witness." Stoicism had its faults, but
it was the noblest in practice of all the Greek schools
of philosophy. Yet the chasm between the Stoic conception of the Divine and the God revealed in Jesus
Christ was so wide that no human power could bridge
it. Stoicism was a doctrine of despair—of a noble
disgust with the vile corruption of the decaying heathen
world—which saw no way of escape but suicide. It
could not regenerate, it could not overcome the world.
Then in the darkest hour the light burst forth. Christ
came, the Light of the world, and with Him joy and
hope and purity were born, for he that saw Him saw
God as He was and is and ever will be.

Philosophy, as the early Christian thinkers perceived,
was a preparation for Christ, inasmuch as throughout
the Roman world it assisted in giving a higher meaning to
the word "God" ($\theta\epsilon\acute{o}s$, *deus*) than it had had in heathen
religions. It also taught the unity of the Universe,
and led to the conviction that in it or behind it there
must exist some Mind and Will. Yet philosophy could
go no further. It could not reveal the Unknown God,
though it might in some minds arouse a yearning for
Him, of Whose existence even Epicurus thought that
man, as man, had an "anticipation" ($\pi\rho\acute{o}\lambda\eta\psi\iota s$). This
very failure of man's efforts to find God was doubtless
one of the chief lessons which the race has had to learn
in the educatory process which we can trace throughout

history. All philosophy everywhere teaches it. " The world by its wisdom knew not God."

Those who, in the Græco-Roman world, rejected the Light when it dawned, and, through pride in their reason, clung to the torches they had themselves kindled, pursued philosophy for centuries. But they made no progress. Neo-Platonism in despair allied itself with the lowest heathenism, against which [philosophy had first risen in protest. It tried to take refuge in magic, Thaumaturgy, Necromancy. But it could not extinguish the True Light that was already shining, and it soon faded away from the minds of men.

We have already referred somewhat briefly to Chinese and Indian philosophy. Of later European philosophy it is unnecessary to say anything except that, many and great as have been the intellects which have devoted themselves to such an interesting subject, it cannot be maintained that they have ever discovered anything more regarding the Nature of God than has been revealed to us by our Lord. Nor have they made God more real, more true, more near, to a single human soul, than does the Gospel of Christ.

In the Muḥammadan world, if anywhere, it might be thought that a " simple Monotheism " might be able to stand, as appealing to man's reason. But experience has shown that, when the doctrine of the Divine Unity is subjected to examination, if that Unity is regarded as Absolute, it leads to Agnosticism or Pantheism. All Muḥammadan philosophy proves this. Hence the rise of the I'tizâl and Ṣûfî schools, of which the latter is almost, if not quite, as Pantheistic as the Indian philosophy by which it has been so largely influenced, and which it so closely resembles in its teaching. It is well known that Jewish philosophy, though starting from the Monotheism of the Old Testament, resolved itself into Agnosticism in Maimonides [1] and into Pantheism in Spinoza. However we may account for it, Christianity has proved itself to be the only faith which in this twentieth century preserves to us a God Whom we can, in some very real degree, know and worship without repudiating either reason or conscience.

[1] Vide ch. vi.

CHAPTER VI

Belief in Divine Incarnations

WE have already recognized a tendency among men to conceive of the gods as magnified human beings. This was in its most common form an evil thing, for it taught men to worship beings gigantic in wickedness. Yet this was the *abuse* of the tendency. Under it lay an instinct not devoid of truth, as we shall see presently. Polytheism brought a multitude of gods and goddesses so near to men that familiarity bred contempt, as we see in Aristophanes and other comedians, and later in Lucian. When refuge was taken in philosophy, the result often was Pantheism and loss of all distinction between good and evil : though Socrates shows, in Plato's dialogue *Euthyphron*, that Polytheism was unable to state what should be thought good and what condemned as bad in human conduct. But whether Pantheism or Agnosticism took the place of Polytheism, in one sense the result was the same. In place of gods near at hand, though often immoral, philosophy, as we have seen, almost necessarily produced a God afar off, a Deity who was often only a mental abstraction, an hypothesis, dim and far away, even when not said to be unconscious, impersonal, devoid of volition, according to many forms of Indian thought. Now with such a Deity men had nothing in common. He had no human attributes, He

was absorbed in the contemplation of His own perfec-
tions, or at any rate He was too great to take any interest
in the sorrows and sufferings of puny creatures like men,
who, from His point of view, were not far removed from
apes.   A Deity of this kind might be very lofty, but He
was too unreal, too unpractical, too remote, to hear men's
prayers.   Man cannot worship an abstraction—which
is one reason why the modern so-called " Religion of
Humanity " has not had any conspicuous success, and
why the worship of " Reason " as a goddess during the
Reign of Terror in France did not produce a new variety
of piety.   In religious matters it is possible to be too
" refined," and such an attenuated conception of a Deity
as philosophy has produced in East and West alike is of
little real assistance to man's mental faculties, and of not
the least satisfaction to the yearnings of his spiritual
instincts.

If men could not draw near to God, it was natural that
they should strive to bring down the Divine to themselves,
to make IT in some way cognisable to the senses.   Hence
came the worship of the sun and moon and other natural
objects, the adoration of fire, of sacred animals, and
finally of images.   Greek philosophy contemptuously
permitted idolatry to the vulgar herd, and, when Christianity came to oppose the worship of idols, philosophy
became their champion and defender.   A philosophical
explanation could be found even for the most foolish
practices and the vilest enormities connected with the
worship of images.   We know how in later times idolatry
invaded the Christian Church, and how even now, not
only in the most corrupt parts of it (where winking
Madonnas and miracle-working *Bambinos* are the order
of the day, inheriting under new names the old heathen

worship), but even in reformed sections of the Church, reverence for " images " and the use of them in devotion has been advocated at Church Congresses.[1] History repeats itself, for those who need nothing of the sort themselves sometimes imitate the philosophers of old and hold that such things are a help to the ignorant. It would be impossible for any one who clung to the authority of Holy Scripture to justify a practice condemned so strongly alike in the Old Testament and in the New ; but, from the very fact of the wide spread of idol worship and its firm grasp of men for many ages, it is not unwise to infer that there must be some cause for it and *some* lesson to be learnt therefrom.

The instinct which, when abused, produces Nature-worship, Polytheism and idolatry, is that which teaches men to seek God, if haply they may " feel after Him and find Him "—the feeling that they need a God near at hand and not far off, a God Who has come to them, Whom they can in some measure know personally as they know their friends, or at least their rulers. The error of philosophy was that it removed God afar off. Idolatry could not fully satisfy men's need, for there must always be something unreal about an idol, even if regarded not as the god himself but only as the representation or the habitation of the god. Life and motion at any rate it could not have, and these two attributes early impressed men as manifestations of the Divine. Animal-worship offered in this way what idolatry could not. If the gods

---

[1] The Principal of a Theological college told the writer that he was inclined to think that, since the Incarnation, idolatry had ceased to be a sin ! But such passages as 1 Cor. vi. 9 ; x. 7 ; Eph. v. 5 ; 1 John v. 21 ; Rev. xxi. 8, 15, refute such an idea.

could manifest themselves as animals, why not as men ?
It may, perhaps, have been in this manner that in different
lands there arose belief in Divine Incarnations. A
human being in whom a deity was incarnate could at
least understand men and be understood by men better
than could an idol or a dumb animal.

It is well known that in early (though not in the very
earliest) times kings were deified in Babylonia. In
Egypt the Pharaohs were regarded as Sons of the Sun,
children or incarnations of Rā'. Egyptian religious
documents are very outspoken : they leave us in no
doubt as to the manner in which the future Pharaoh was
said to have been conceived. Goodness, holiness of life,
virtue, mercy, justice, piety—none of these qualities
were necessary for the " divine " Pharaoh in Egypt, nor
for such incarnate divinities elsewhere in the ancient
world. Krishna is an example in point. It is by no
means certain that he ever lived as a man, but the Hindû
Purânas speak of him as an incarnation of Vishṇu. His
character, as described in the Purâṇas, is one long catalogue of murder and adultery ; none the less he is the
favourite deity of India to-day, and men are urged to the
" Imitation of Krishṇa." The Indian doctrine of the
Avatâras [1] or " Descents " of Vishṇu represents him as
more frequently incarnating himself in animal than in
human form. The Pantheism which underlies all Indian
religious thought, coupled with belief in Transmigration
and the consequent sacredness of all life, rendered this
easy. The separation of morality from religion prevented
men from feeling any revulsion at the idea of worshipping

---

[1] It is, of course, quite possible that the doctrine of the Avatâras
may be much more recent than the beginning of the Christian
era.

such a being as the immoral Kṛishṇa, just as the tales of Zeus' amours rendered him none the less worthy of worship in the opinion of the great mass of the ancient Greeks.

We have already said, and we say it again, that in no heathen system of religion—in fact in *no* religion known to us except Christianity and its earlier stage of Biblical Judaism—can there be found the conception of *Holiness* as God's most essential attribute. It is taught throughout the Bible, but nowhere else. Hence the various heathen " incarnations," of whatever deity, were not holy, nor did their lack of that quality in the very slightest degree detract from their Divine claims in the opinion of their worshippers. We see the same thing in Islâm in more recent times, whenever deity has been claimed by any heretical sect for its founder. The most noteworthy instance of this is the case of the deified Chiefs of the Ismâ'îlians or " Assassins," but the same may be said of the worship of 'Alî by the 'Alî-ilâhîs, and of the Bâb and Bahâ in our own times.

We have seen that a true instinct abused led to Nature-worship, idolatry, and belief that some god or other was incarnate in a Pharaoh, a sacred bull, or such a being as Kṛishṇa. If we remove the abuse, we find that this instinct reveals humanity as yearning for a human manifestation of the Divine, and unable to find satisfaction in corrupt and sinful men who represented unholy gods. Are we hence to conclude that this almost universal longing for a self-revelation of God was wrong and unmeaning ? Or is it more reasonable to infer that the desire was implanted *that it might be satisfied,* and that the Holy One was preparing men and educating them, even by their failure to find satisfaction in idolatry and in the worship of false incarnations, to accept the true Incarnation when revealed in the Person of Christ? This is certainly the Christian view of the matter.

It is here that the Doctrine of the Trinity in Unity comes in to remove intellectual difficulties. We cannot enter into this subject now, except very briefly to point out the difficulty which in three systems of absolute Monotheism has made men feel that it was an impossibility ever to know God, because He could not reveal Himself to His creatures. Students of Maimonides, the eminent Jewish writer of the Middle Ages (A.D. 1135–1204), will remember that he holds that God's Oneness excludes His possession of all attributes, because that would imply a kind of plurality; or at least he argues that God is not wise through wisdom or mighty through having might, and that between what is called mercy, love, and goodness in man and the same attributes in God there is no likeness. God, this Jewish philosopher teaches, is best described by negatives, e.g., by saying that He is immortal, devoid of body, not liable to pain or injury, and so on. "Orthodox" Muslim theology has arrived at much the same conclusion. The result is that absolute Monotheism enables men to know what God is *not*, instead of knowing what He *is*. Unitarianism among ourselves is driven to the same form of Agnosticism. In the Shí'ite sect of Islâm, dominant in Persia, an attempt to avoid this has been made by the invention of the doctrine of the necessity of there always being among men an Imâm ("leader") or Bâb ("gate"), able to reveal God's will. Sûfî thought asserts the existence of beings termed the First Unveiling (*Tajallî*), the Second Unveiling (or Shining forth, i.e., Manifestation) of the ONE, and so on. This is not unlike the Æons of the Gnostics, the " Second God " of Philo, Plato's secondary Deity incorporate in the Universe, and many other such speculations. We are also reminded of the Archetypal Man (*Âdâm Qadmôn*) of Hebrew speculation, and the *Logos*-theory found in some sort in the Targums (there styled in Aramaic *Mêymrâ* with the same meaning of " The Word ") as well as in Plato and Philo. In the Preface to his Gospel, St. John clearly shows that Christ fulfils, and more than fulfils, all that reason and speculation had made men recognize as necessary to a Divine self-revelation, and that He was not only the Logos but the Life, the Son of God. " And the Logos became flesh and dwelt among us (and we beheld His glory, the glory as of the Only-Begotten of the Father) full of grace and truth." This at once shows the truth which underlay idol-worship, the adoration of supposed incarnations, and philosophic speculations, and at the same time satisfies man's desire for a revelation of the Invisible God, Whom he has been feeling after, like one groping in the darkness.

It has well been said by a recent writer [1] :—

If there is any personal expression or manifestation of God at all within our world, it can be only in and through a person or persons. . . . God cannot manifest Himself in mere Nature, either in the whole or in any particular fact or phenomenon of it. Because " Himself " means His Personality, and there is nowhere in Nature, as such, any " self " or " self-hood " that can manifest or express personality . . . God reveals Himself in a Person in Whom Himself, His personal Self, can be, and be seen. . . . In all the actual Universe, so far as we know or can know it, God is nowhere directly knowable save in the Person of Jesus Christ.

There is no room for theory in this matter, for we have the Fact of Christ and the fact that in Him, and in Him

[1] Du Bose, *The Reason of Life*, pp. 205, 207.

alone, have men—some of every race, time and clime—risen to the conception of a Deity Whom they can in a measure truly know, love and trust. Every child of man can, if he will, test this for himself and learn its truth by his own experience. No other system of religion has ever been known to satisfy men's deepest needs : their conceptions of God have been too base and material. No philosophical system has succeeded, for they all give too " rarefied " and unreal an idea of God, or explain Him away as a theory, an abstraction. There is nothing low or base, nothing abstract or unreal, in the Jesus of the Evangelists. The Incarnation of the Word of God is proved by the historical facts on which Christianity rests, as has been already said. The Incarnation reveals God, and shows what man should be and will ultimately become. It explains the meaning of conscience and justifies what Kant calls its " Categorical Imperative." It gives men a motive-power for self-denial, self-restraint, self-conquest, and for love towards and effort for the good of their fellow-men. It sanctifies manhood and dignifies " the body of our humiliation." The practical result of this from a moral point of view is forcibly stated by Sir J. R. Seeley in these words [1] :—

Compare the ancient with the modern world : " Look on this picture and on that." One broad distinction in the characters of men forces itself into prominence. Among all the men of the ancient heathen world there were scarcely one or two to whom we might venture to apply the epithet, " holy." In other words, there were not more than one or two, if any, who, besides being virtuous in their actions, were possessed with an unaffected enthusiasm of goodness, and, besides abstaining from vice, regarded even a vicious thought with horror. Probably no one will deny that in

---

[1] " Ecce Homo," end of ch. xv.

Christian countries this higher-toned goodness, which we call holiness, has existed. Few will maintain that it has been exceedingly rare. Perhaps the truth is, that there has scarcely been a town in any Christian country since the time of Christ where a century has passed without exhibiting a character of such elevation that his mere presence has shamed the bad and made the good better, and has been felt at times like the presence of God Himself. And if this be so, has Christ failed ? or can Christianity die ? . . . The conception of morality which Christ gave has now become the universal one, and no man is thought good who does not in some measure satisfy it. . . . The story of His life will always remain the one record in which the moral perfection of man stands revealed in its root and its unity, the hidden spring made palpably manifest by which the whole machine is moved.[1]

Before concluding this part of the subject it may be well to notice two other points connected therewith. One is the Modernist fancy that there is no need to insist on the historicity of the Christ of the Gospels, that the Ideal is true, and that this is enough and even better than the actual historical existence of such a character. In reply it may be said that, if we for the sake of argument grant for the moment that the Evangelists have drawn an ideal rather than a truthful picture of our Lord and theirs, then it is remarkable that such an ideal should have occurred to such men. Nothing else like it is found in all literature before or since.[2] The man who could draw such an ideal picture would be a miracle. Were it possible to accept such a baseless theory, the Christian faith would be a mere castle in the air, and would melt away like a dream, leaving us hopeless and helpless to the stern and cruel realities of a world without God. You cannot build a true religion on ideals, however beautiful, any more than an actual city on the mirage of the

[1] Op. cit., concluding chapter.
[2] Vide my *Religio Critici*, ch. ii.

beautifully wooded shore of a lake, seen amid the desert sands. Both lake and city must be real to exist under such conditions. Men have long sought for, and in Christ's City of God have found, " the city which hath the foundations," nor, if they are wise, will they forsake it to seek elsewhere for any fabled or fancied El Dorado. Fact is preferable to fiction. The actual Christ, instead of falling short of the picture His disciples have drawn of Him, doubtless surpassed it in every perfection. Here the actual was grander, truer, nobler, than any human ideal could ever be.

The other suggestion is that the doctrine of the Incarnation was originally a heathen idea, borrowed by the Jews, and developed into the Christian belief on the subject. But surely this is hardly correct. The heathen view was that certain imperfect men, or whole classes of men, such as the Pharaohs, often monsters of wickedness, were incarnations of unholy gods. But there are no unholy gods : there is no God but One, the Most Holy. To us, nowadays, the idea of an unholy God is a contradiction in terms. The teaching of Christ Himself, the One Perfect Man, the acknowledged Head and Teacher of the human race, is that God is Holy, and that whosoever has seen the Christ has seen God. That the Perfect Man should reveal the Perfect God as clearly as it is possible for men to behold Him is by no means incredible in itself. It becomes not only credible but certain when it is asserted by Christ. Experience shows that all men can love and worship and serve the God revealed in Christ, if they will, and can rise to a higher life, even here, by doing so. It also shows that for us in the twentieth century, and for the awakening nations of the East also, when the picture of the actual Christ of the Gospels is fairly brought before

G

them, the choice remains, as we have already said, either to worship the God revealed in Him, or to reject religion altogether.   This is a very serious fact, the dread significance of which is not always fully grasped.   Does it not show that truth underlay even heathen ideas of incarnations, and that their imperfect guesses have been at once justified and corrected in the Incarnation of the Son of the Living God ?

CHAPTER VII

Virgin Birth

DURING the last few years a great deal has been written upon this subject, and conclusions reached which are worthy of an age of theory and hasty generalization. That is to say, in matters of religion and theology, at all events, men are far too apt to accept as correct statements which they have not tested, and to which they are attracted by the fancy that they are new. *New* and *true* are not quite synonymous ; but, if they were, these supposed new ideas are, in many cases, " as old as the hills," so to speak. They have been refuted and exploded centuries since, and so completely disproved that most men have never even heard of them. Hence their apparent newness in our eyes is merely because of our ignorance. Antiquity of error cannot be thus transformed into newness of truth.

The " man in the street," if he thinks about this subject at all, assures us that, " of all old-world legends " none is so common as that of " a virgin-born, or in some way divinely-born, Saviour." Hence he concludes that, even in the Christian religion, there is no ground for accepting such a doctrine. The fact that, in his opinion, men of many other religions have believed much the same renders it clear that the Christian tenet is as baseless as he concludes that of other faiths to be on this point.   Such a dogma, he holds, must have come into Christianity from some heathen source.   He has been gravely assured that certain Australian tribes practically hold *all* births to be virgin-births, that at one time " doubt-less " this opinion was general among men, and that it has survived in special instances in the form of a theologi-cal dogma.   Therefore, " liberality of thought " requires him to think the whole thing an absurdity, for, he is assured, the same belief prevailed at one time about Horus, the Pharaohs, Fo-hi, Buddha, Zoroaster and three of his descendants, Perseus and many other Greek heroes, Plato, Alexander the Great, Kṛishṇa, Mithra, and many other gods, demigods, and great men.

Now all this is a labyrinth of error, " confusion worse confounded."   There is a vast difference, to begin with, between Virgin-birth and any other " supernatural " method of birth.   The former, we shall see, hardly ever, *if ever*, was believed to have occurred in any religion but the Christian, though in the Christian faith it has from the beginning been held with regard to one Person, and only one Person, in the whole world.   Supernatural occurrences in some form are, on the contrary, stated, truly or falsely, to have attended the conception of most men in the ancient world who, in the realm of fact or in that of fable, surpassed the great mass in some remark-able way.   To confound these two things, Virgin-birth and supernatural birth, with one another is not conducive to clearness of thought.   For example, Muslim tradition relates many marvels regarding Muḥammad's birth, and at his conception it is said that the " Light of Muḥam-mad," which had shone on Adam's forehead and on that of each of Muḥammad's ancestors' up to that time, left his father 'Abdu'llâh and attended his mother Âminah until

Muḥammad's birth, when it attached itself to him. Here, of course, we have an ancient Persian myth, originally relating to Jamshîd (Yima-Khshaêta, " shining Yima "), transferred to Muḥammad. But the Muslims have never dreamt of asserting that their " Prophet " was Virgin-born. On the other hand they admit (in the Qur'ân itself) that *Christ* was. . Here we have an instance of the vast difference between two things which many people nowadays confound with one another. After much study of the subject I am in a position to state that Virgin-birth was believed of *not one* of the real or imaginary characters mentioned in the list given above. This view I now proceed to give good evidence for accepting, though it will be easily understood that I am precluded from writing in plain English much that is clearly stated in the original authorities to which reference has ultimately to be made.

It must be remembered that Greeks as well as Egyptians (and other nations) believed that their deities had material bodies. Hence it is that Homer tells how some of them were wounded, even by mortal heroes, with material spears, and how from their wounds flowed the *ichor* which in the gods supplies the place of blood. Nor must it be forgotten that in some cases we have in mythology what were originally allegorical accounts of the life and growth of plants. Thus, not unfrequently, as we have seen, the sky is the father, the earth is the fruitful mother, and the vital germs are the rain-drops. These things are material enough, and certainly convey no idea of Virgin-birth.

Remembering all this, we turn to Egypt in the first place and enquire what foundation there is for the modern oft-repeated assertion that in that land Horus was said to have been born of the " Virgin Isis." There are many stories about Isis and Horus, and Horus the elder has to be distinguished from Horus the younger and from others of the name. Here is one of these tales as given by Professor Maspero [1] :—

Isis, the cow,[2] or woman with cow's horns, had not always belonged to him (Osiris). Originally she was an independent deity, dwelling at Buto in the midst of the ponds of Adhu. She had neither husband or lover, but had spontaneously conceived and given birth to a son, whom she suckled among the reeds—a lesser Horus, who was called Ḥar-si-îsît, " Horus the son of Isis," to distinguish him from Haroêris. At an early period she was married to her neighbour Osiris, and no marriage could have been better suited to her nature. For she personified the earth— not the earth in general, like Sibu, with its unequal distribution of seas and mountains, deserts and cultivated land—but the black and luxuriant plain of the Delta, where races of men, plants and animals increase and multiply in ever-succeeding generations. To whom did she owe this inexhaustible productive energy, if not to her neighbour Osiris, the Nile ? The Nile rises, overflows, lingers upon the soil ; every year it is wedded to the Earth, and the Earth comes forth green and fruitful from its embraces. The marriage of the two elements suggested that of the two divinities. Osiris wedded Isis and adopted the young Horus.

To represent the Delta as a fruitful cow and to say that its soil at first brought forth produce without being flooded by the Nile, but afterwards needed such an overflow of water to make it fruitful, and to worship Earth and Nile and the personified products of the

---

[1] *The Dawn of Civilization*, pp. 131–132.

[2] In Apuleius (*Metamorphoses*, Lib. xi., 2), she is called " Queen of Heaven," and identified with Ceres, the heavenly Venus, Proserpina, and other goddesses : see also cap. 5. In her procession, after Anubis there followed a cow standing erect, " the fruitful image of the all-parent goddess." The worship of Isis was attended with much immorality. She was goddess of fertility, not of virginity. These things are *not quite* the same, though some modern mythologists seem to think that they are.

teeming soil, were things natural in ancient Egypt. But it is doubtful whether there is much of Virgin-birth, or rather of heifer-birth, to be found in such a tale. In Plutarch's time the Egyptians explained[1] Osiris as the Nile, Isis as the Earth, and Horus as "the season and temperature of the surrounding air, preserving and nourishing everything," and adds that Horus sprang "from the *union* of Nile and Earth."

In the *Book of the Dead* Horus is given more than one father, and nothing whatever is said of his Virgin-birth. Dr. Budge states that Isis is represented as raising up the body of Osiris after his murder, as "being united to him," and as thus conceiving and giving birth to Horus.[2] Plutarch's account agrees with this and goes into details regarding both the younger[3] and the elder Horus.[4] Into these we dare not follow him. Suffice it to say that they completely confute the modern talk about the "Virgin" Isis.

We have already seen that the Pharaohs were styled Sons of Rā', the Sun-god. But Egyptian documents state in unmistakable language exactly how they became such. One such papyrus tells us that the god Amon (often identified with Rā') transformed himself into the royal person of Thuthmosis II, in order that the queen might conceive.[5] The story of Amon-Ḥotep's conception

---

[1] *De Iside et Osiride*, capp. 32, 33, 38.

[2] Introd. to Version of *Book of the Dead*, p. lxxx.

In a Hymn to Osiris, it is said that, when Isis found Osiris' dead body, "aquam eius extraxit, heredem fecit."

[3] *De Iside et Osiride*, cap. 19.

[4] Op. cit., cap. 12.

[5] Those who know even a little of Egyptian may read for themselves the *full particulars* in the hieroglyphic text, printed pp. 101, sqq. of Adolf Erman's *Ægyptische Chrestomathie*, 1904.

is given in another similar document, and it is there said that the god Amon Rā' had "incarnated himself in the *royal person* of this husband," Thuthmosis IV, in order to bring this about. Supernatural birth was, therefore, in a measure asserted of the Pharaohs, but it was most emphatically not *Virgin*-birth.

Turning now to China, we find some curious tales told of Fo-hi (also called Fû-hsi), the mythical founder of the Chinese Empire, in the thirty-fourth century before the Christian era. One of these stories is that his mother went to bathe, and on returning she found a flower lying on her clothes. This she ate, and Fo-hi's birth finally resulted therefrom. Another version of the tale has it [1] that, walking by the bank of a river one day, she trod in a giant's footprint. She was then encircled by a rainbow. After twelve years' pregnancy she bore a son with a dragon's body. Another account said he had a bull's head and a serpent's body. Those who know the East and Eastern ways of speaking and writing are not likely to consider that this conveys to the Chinese mind any suggestion of *Virgin*-birth. Prof. H. A. Giles, Professor of Chinese at Oxford, says [2] distinctly that there is no mention of Virgin-birth in the case of Fo-hi.

The ancestor of the Chinese royal house of Chow is a personage named Hou Chi (or How Tsih), who is said to have lived in the reign of the Emperor Shun (B.C. 2255–2205). The Chow dynasty ascended the throne B.C. 1122, more than a thousand years after his death. Hou Chi, as their ancestor, then received high honour,

---

[1] Sergius Georgievski, *Pervwiy Period Kitayskoy Istoriy*, p. 7.
[2] *Pagan and Christian Parallels*, p. 46.

and sacrifices were offered to him. The following Ode is said[1] to have then been composed and sung in his honour :—

> [2] She who gave birth to our people
> Was the lady Chiang Yüan.
> How did she give birth to them ?
> She offered up a sacrifice
> That she might not be childless :
> Then she trod in a footprint of God's, and conceived
> The great and blessed one,
> Pregnant with a new birth to be,
> And brought forth and nourished
> Him who was Hou Chi.

Here it should be noticed that " in the legend of her son's conception and birth, which is given in the first stanza of this Ode, while evidently they were believed to be miraculous, it is somewhat doubtful whether we are to translate *Ti* in the sixth line by ' God,' or by ' Emperor ' (meaning her husband)."[3] Certainly *Ti* is a term which by itself (as here used) does not denote the Supreme God (Shang-Ti) of the Chinese. It means rather " a god," just as in a heathen Latin, or Greek, or Sanskrit author *deus*, θεος, or *deva* would. As the translator says, it may here refer to the Emperor Kuh, whose princess consort the mother of Hou Chi is said to have been, though there are chronological difficulties in the way. But these may not have troubled an Oriental poet writing more than a thousand years later. What settles the matter, however, is the statement that Chiang Yüan " offered up a sacrifice that she might not be

[1] Jenning's *Shi King*, p. 294. The ode is in Pt. iii., Bk. ii., No. 1, of that work.
[2] Dr. Giles' *Religions of Ancient China*, p. 21.
[3] Jennings, op. cit., p. 294.

childless." Maidens do not generally do that. Such
a statement shows that, in the poet's opinion, she was
already married and had for some time in vain hoped
for offspring.

The same kind of tale as that told about Fo-hi is
told also of the ancestor of the Manchu Dynasty. His
mother ate a red fruit instead of a flower. What
has been said of the original tale applies to this
also.

Some of the most vivid imaginations of our day have
been exercised with the object of proving that belief in
Virgin-birth has repeatedly asserted itself in Indian
legend. Occasionally this has been " proved " up to
the hilt by the simple and straightforward process of
re-writing these Indian myths, thus making them say
what European opponents of Christianity think they
ought to say, but what, unfortunately, no Hindû writer
ever fancied in connexion with them. Jacolliot, Schuré,
Marius and others have adopted this ingenious, if not
exactly ingenuous, method of misleading people unac-
quainted with their practically unlimited mendacity.
But as this has been sufficiently exposed by such an
authority as Professor de Harlez,[1] it is unnecessary to
dwell upon it further. We proceed to take the chief
instances in which Virgin-birth is by some still asserted
to be affirmed of certain real or mythical personages
in Indian writings, and to enquire to what extent this
dogma is really taught about them and believed in by
their adherents. Of course this must be done very
briefly.

Krishna is the first of these asserted Indian instances
of supposed Virgin-birth. When we remember that

[1] *Vedisme, Brahmanisme et Christianisme.*

the Purânas which contain Krishna's " history " are
of uncertain date but were all certainly composed at
earliest several centuries after the beginning of our era,
and that the same thing is true of the Mahâbhârata
(including the Bhagavad Gîtâ, which is an episode in that
great epic poem) it will be clear that, even if they did
contain the statement that Krishna was born of a virgin,
this could not be supposed to be a belief of purely Indian
origin. But they do nothing of the sort. The Bhâgavata Purâna teaches that, so far from being a virgin,
Devakî, Krishna's mother, had before him borne her
husband, Vasudeva, no less than *seven* children. It is
hardly necessary to pursue the subject further. Suffice
it to say that *no* Indian authorities, not even quite modern
Hindû writers [1] who have composed books in English
in laudation of Krishna, have ever attempted to assert
his Virgin-birth. Yet this is not due to any desire to
impose as little as possible upon their readers' credulity,
for Muralidhur Râya casually mentions [2] that the infant
Krishna, when sucking, " yawned, and revealed to his
wondering mother the entire universe in his little mouth."
A student of philosophy called " Krishna, the son of
Devakî " is mentioned—without further details—in the
Chhândogya Upanishad,[3] but the later Brâhmans seem
to have made no attempt to identify him with the Krishna,
son of Devakî and Vasudeva, who is now the most popular
god in India.

Some modern European writers have boldly asserted
that Buddhists believe that the founder of their faith,

---

[1] As, for instance, Hirendra Nâth Datta, Balarâma Mallika,
Muralidhur Râya, etc.

[2] *Sree Krishna*, p. 17.

[3] iii., § 17, 6. See below, p. 156, note.

the Indian philosopher Buddha, was born of a Virgin, Mâyâ by name. The origin of this fancy among Europeans is curious. It seems to come from some words of Jerome, who says that the Indian Gymnosophists had a tradition that Buddha was born from a virgin's side.[1] There *is* a late Buddhist myth that he sprang from Mâyâ's side, but the question of her virginity is another matter. Jerome got this idea, in all probability, from the claim made for himself by Terebinthus, a Persian (?) impostor, who, long after the beginning of the Christian era,[2] took the name of Buddha upon himself, and said he was born of a virgin and of God the Father, meaning by the latter a sage called Scythianus [3] of Saracen descent, who had taught him his heresy. This man Terebinthus showed that he was borrowing from Christian sources by choosing out twelve disciples for himself. Deceived by the fact that Terebinthus called himself Buddha, Jerome seems to have confounded him with the Indian sage of that title, and hence to have wrongly attributed to Buddhist *Samanas*, or ascetics, the belief in Buddha's Virgin-birth, which was directly contrary to their tenets. Modern European writers of a certain " school of thought " have plunged much more deeply into the mire, and have stated that the *Indian* Buddha had twelve disciples, whereas it was the *Persian* Buddha, Terebinthus, who in that respect *imitated* our Lord designedly some centuries after His birth.

[1] *Contra Jovinianum*, Lib. i., § 22.

[2] Possibly about A.D. 200, as Mânî was born about 215 and was put to death about 276 A.D.

[3] Vide Cyril of Jerusalem's *Catechesis VI*, and Reischls' note (from Petrus Siculus) on cap. 25 : Photius, *Hist. Manichæorum* : Archelai Disputatio cum Manichæo, cap. 52 : Theodoret, Hær. Fabb., i., 26.

As for Mâyâ's virginity, the early Pâli books which form the Scriptures of the Buddhists of the Southern School (called also *Hînâyâna*) have not the very faintest suggestion of such a thing. Professor Rhys Davids considers from the data which they supply that she must have been " about the forty-fifth year of her age " when " she promised her husband a son." It is highly probable that she had been married about the age of twelve, or even earlier, in accordance with Indian custom, and *had been a wife for some thirty-three years*. In the *Mahâvamsa*, the earliest part of which is said to date from the fifth century of our era, it is written thus : " Mâyâ and Pajâpatî both equally became the consorts of Suddhodano. Our Vanquisher " (i.e. Buddha) " was the son of the Mahârâjâ Suddhodano and of Mâyâ." [1] This shows clearly that in " Orthodox " Southern Buddhism no belief in Mâyâ's virginity then existed. Nor has that tenet yet been accepted there. In Northern Buddhism it is very doubtful if it has ever existed either. Some fancy they can detect it in Ašvaghosha's *Buddha-charita*, which was translated into Chinese early in the fifth century of the Christian era, and may have been written some centuries earlier. After careful study of the passage in question, I feel very doubtful whether the poet meant anything of the kind, and the Chinese translators clearly were of opinion that he did not. Professor de la Vallée Poussin holds that the doctrine of Buddha's Virgin-birth is contained *only* in the Mahâvastu, a Sanskrit book which is outside the Buddhist canon, is of late date, and from which were ultimately developed the peculiar views of the Northern or Mahâyâna School, now established in Tibet and China. But as this doctrine

[1] Vol. i., cap. 2, verse 10, šl. 11.

has *not* taken root in these countries, it is fairly evident that Buddhists there did not understand the poetic language of the Mahâvastu as teaching anything of the kind. In fact in this book the future Buddha says, "This King Šuddhodana [is to be] my worthy father. He seeks [as my] mother her who may be both kind and high-born and bright of limb and slow of passion and short-lived." [1]

The earlier Buddhist Scriptures recognize nothing remarkable about Buddha's conception. Later, in the Introduction to the Pâli Jâtakas, we find a *dream* of Mâyâ's that a great white elephant entered her side. In later Sanskrit books, for instance in Ašvaghosha's work already mentioned, this dream is spoken of as a reality. Hence in Burma a white elephant is to this day sacred to Buddha. But this does not quite amount to belief in Virgin-birth. We may therefore, safely dismiss the idea that this tenet belongs to Buddhism in any age or in any form. But, if it be thought that the ambiguous language of the Mahâvastu may possibly be taken in support of the theory of Buddha's Virgin-birth, it is at least clear that the idea arose long after Buddha's time and after the first preaching of the Gospel in India, which can be traced back in all probability to a time before the end of the first century.

Attempts have been made to prove that the Mithraists believed in Mithra's Virgin-birth. As we have no Mithraic scriptures extant, an appeal has to be made to the Sanskrit and Avestic books which speak of that deity, and the myths current concerning him in India and Persia before the rise of Mithraism proper. Besides this, certain Greek and Latin writers, heathen and

[1] Senart's ed., vol. ii., p. 2, lines 18, *sqq.* : Paris, 1890.

Christian, have left us some fragmentary information on the subject of Mithraic beliefs and practices. From the study of these authorities [1] and the numerous Mithraic inscriptions and sculptures found in many parts of Europe, we learn that Mithra was a Sun-god pure and simple, and that his adorers in all ages and countries recognized this and styled him the " Unconquered Sun." He was not believed to have ever lived on earth as a human being, and every attempt to find even the shadow of a shade of proof that his worshippers imagined a birth from a Virgin in connexion with him has therefore naturally failed. Inscriptions and written documents agree in stating that Mithra sprang from a rock, and sculptures represent this scene. The meaning of this is evident when we remember that the word for " rock " in Avestic Persian (*asman*) and in Sanskrit (*ašman*) also means " cloud " and " sky." Every day his worshippers therefore witnessed his birth with their own eyes, and he was worshipped in caves cut out in the rock to express the same fact. If we go back to the Avesta, the sacred book of the Zoroastrians, we find that, before the rise of Mithraism in its Western form, much the same idea prevailed in Persia, for he is there spoken of as one of the sons of Ahura Mazdâ (Ôrmazd) and Speñta Ârmaiti, the latter being one of Ahura Mazdâ's daughters and the tutelary *goddess of the earth*. This is what is referred to by an Armenian writer who speaks of the Persians as holding that " The god Mithra was *incestuously* born of a mortal mother." This passage has been taken as

[1] Vide my *Mythic Christs and the True*, and my Victoria Institute paper on " Mithraism," in *Journal of Transactions*, vol. xliii., pp. 237, *sqq.*

a proof of belief in Virgin-birth! Can imaginative ingenuity go further?

We have recently been assured that the followers of Zoroaster believed not only that this great reformer had been born of a Virgin mother, but that three future prophets would come into the world in the same miraculous manner. This statement is quite devoid of foundation, or at least the only foundation it has is ignorance of Persian ideas about the relation between the sexes. As has well been said, " The idea of celibacy is entirely repugnant to the Iranian system (as far as we may judge from the Avesta) and probably also to the tenets of the Achaemenid religion," that is to the faith of Darius and his successors. The Avesta traces Zoroaster's descent back for ten generations, and most distinctly states that his father was a man who bore the name Pôurushaspa,[1] to whom his son was born to reward him for his abundant libations of *haoma*-juice. The name of Zoroaster's mother does not seem to occur[2] in the Avesta, of so little consequence was she in the eyes of the various authors to whom the different parts of that book are due. Later writers call her Dughdhôva, which was further shortened into Dogdo. We are told that Ôrmazd had placed Zoroaster's soul (*fravashi*) in some *haoma*-juice. Pôuruhaspa drank this, and in due course Dughdhôva conceived her son. Later still it is stated that Zoroaster was the *third*[3] of five brothers. Thus the question of Virgin-birth in his case vanishes. The *Bûndahishnîh* (xxxii. 2) says: " By Pôrûshasp was

[1] Vendidad, xix., 6, cf. vv. 6 and 46; Yasht v., 18; xxiii., 4; xxiv., 2; Yasna, ix., 13.

[2] If we except a fragment quoted by Bartholemä.

Zad Sparam, xv., 5.

Zaratûsht begotten for a sanctuary of the good religion."
Even when the *Zarâtusht-nâmah* was composed, in A.D.
1278, to exalt Zoroaster in every possible way, not a
word occurs in it to support the theory of Virgin-birth.
Nor have the Pârsîs, even up to the present day, borrowed
this dogma or developed it.

With regard to the three prophets for whose coming
the Zoroastrians looked, expecting them to be born
with an interval of a thousand years between each one
and his predecessor, the same may be said. They were
to be sprung from Zoroaster, though by three different
mothers. Details are given in the books of the Pârsîs
to explain exactly how these three men, born so long
after Zoroaster's death, were yet to be *his own sons* (cf.
Bûndahishnîh, xxxii. 8, 9), but we have not the courage
to quote them here. Suffice it to say that, strange as
is the story, it does not in any way imply Virgin-birth
in the case of any one of the three. In Persia no such
belief existed, being opposed to the whole spirit of the
Zoroastrian faith.

In the second (or early in the third) [1] century of our
era, a fierce attack on the Christian faith was
made by a Greek writer named Celsus, on the ground
that the Christian teaching with regard to our Lord's
Virgin-birth was practically identical with what the
Greek fables taught regarding Perseus, Æacus, Minos,
Amphion and others of their real or mythical heroes.
Origen answered this attack at full length. And our
present knowledge of other mythologies besides that of
the Greeks enables us to examine and refute the same
charge when revived in our own days in the extended
form in which we have been considering it. Suffice it

---

[1] More probably between 170 and 180 A.D.

H

to say here that the Greek myths about these heroes did not ascribe to them anything that could be called *Virgin*-birth. Zeus and the other Greek deities were always very material, whether in their own proper forms, as has been already pointed out, or when metamorphosed into a shower of gold, a bull, a man, or something else equally tangible. Nature-myths are not always pleasant things to study in all their details. Some of these Greek stories can hardly have ever been intended to be taken literally, at least in the form in which they have come down to us. The story of Perseus is well known. It does not merely consist of the incident of the visit of Zeus to the imprisoned Danaê in the form of a shower of gold, and her consequent conception, but proceeds to tell of the magic mirror, the cap which rendered Perseus invisible, the brazen hands of the Gorgons, the clever manner in which the hero avoided the danger of being turned into stone, and how he cut off Medusa's head with a sickle. Fairy-tales among all nations have been collected and compared with the Legend of Perseus. Now fairy tales sometimes contain much that is interesting, and fragments of ancient mythology may often be discovered in some of them. But it is by no means unusual now to invent or improve upon them for the amusement of our children, and we are not forbidden to suppose that the same custom existed in ancient times also. At any rate, when writers coolly propose to compare the Legend of Perseus with the records regarding our Lord, we must ask them not to omit every incident but one in their Legend. Let them bring in the " Tarn-kappe " and all the rest.

We are occasionally reminded that in ancient times tales were circulated about the birth of Plato, Alexander the Great, and certain other distinguished persons, and these are adduced to show how " widespread " was belief in " Virgin-birth." Here again, however, the phantom vanishes when approached a little closer and called by its right name. In no single case is Virgin-birth asserted or implied about such men, certainly not about either of the two above mentioned. Plutarch (*Sympos.*, Bk. viii., ch. i.), Diogenes Laërtius, and Jerome, refer to a story that Perictionê, Plato's mother, received a visit from Apollo in human form. But all these writers lived after the beginning of the Christian era, and they neither gave credence to the tale themselves nor give any reason to think that any of Plato's disciples did so. At any rate those who told the tale made no attempt to convey the impression of Virgin-birth. So too with regard to Alexander, who is said to have claimed descent from Jupiter Ammon. Plutarch says in his *Life of Alexander* that the mother of the latter used jokingly to complain that her son was trying to embroil her with Juno (Hêrê). She had been the wife of Philip of Macedon for a considerable time before her son's birth.

It is hardly necessary to pursue this subject further. Proverbially difficult as it is to prove an universal negative, we may at least say that we have in vain sought a single instance in which belief in Virgin-birth is taught in any religion but the Christian, even when in later times heathen faiths had every opportunity of borrowing it from Christianity.

That the doctrine should be quite in accordance with reason in our Lord's case, though not in any other, it is not difficult to understand. The character of Christ was quite unique, His modern opponents themselves being judges. His life was unique, His death, resurrection and ascension were unique, and it was quite fitting that His birth should have been unique too. The testimony upon which these things all alike rest is unimpeachable, as the most rigid investigation all through nineteen centuries has shown.

Upon the question of Virgin-birth, then, Comparative Religion sheds no light, except in the sense that it makes the fact evident that this doctrine, far from having been "universal among mankind" at one time, cannot be proved to have been found in any religion but the Christian at any time whatever, and that therefore the doctrine as taught in the Gospel cannot have been borrowed, consciously or unconsciously, from any other faith.

CHAPTER VIII

The Christian and the non-Christian Outlook on Life

THE question, " What is Life ? Has it an object, a purpose, and, if so, what ? " is one that from very early times has forced itself upon thoughtful men everywhere. Certain facts were clear—for instance, that life was very uncertain, that it might terminate at any moment, that in it there must inevitably be some, and might be much, pain, sorrow, disappointment. Of what use then was it ? How should it be made the most of before it vanished away ? Was it intended for pleasure ? Had duty any part in it ? Did God or the gods care what we did with it ? The answers to such questions vary very much in form, but, whether given by religions or by philosophies, they may be readily divided into two classes, the non-Christian and the Christian. The difference between these is great.

The non-Christian view in the past has been, and in the present still is, far from being a cheerful and inspiring one. Maeterlinck evidently imagines that life is meaningless in an aimless Universe. Buddha considered existence the greatest of evils, and extinction, in the first place of all human feelings and in the second of existence itself, the one thing to be aimed at, though a thing almost infinitely difficult of attainment. He could suggest no purpose in life, and therefore condemned all action as likely to lead to a prolongation of a purposeless existence in this or in some other world. This he regarded as an evil, because he taught that all existence, of whatever sort it be, is misery. The Greek sage, Solon, is reported to have said that it was a happy thing to die, but far happier never to have been born. This fairly sums up the general idea of thoughtful Greeks ; for their belief in a dim, shadowy existence after death gave them little comfort and led them to regard life on earth as infinitely preferable, however full of suffering it might be. So-crates, it is true, thought that suicide was wrong, because a soldier should not desert his post until the general ordered him elsewhere. But even he could not see any very clear object in life.

Whether there was or was not any purpose in human life, of one thing the Greeks and Romans had no real doubt—that all things were ruled by blind, relentless fate. There is some question whether Æschylus viewed fate as superior to Zeus or not, but fate, it was generally held, ruled both gods and men. Exactly the same belief prevails among Hindûs to the present day. What is " written on a man's forehead " cannot be altered and must unavoidably come to pass. In the Muḥammadan world the irresistible sway of fate is well known. All that was to occur from the beginning to the end was, Muslim tradition tells us, written down at God's com-mand, by the Pen He had created, upon a " Preserved Tablet " at the foot of God's throne above the highest heaven, ages before the creation of the world. Even the extent of the movement of every single leaf on a tree shaken by the wind is there recorded beforehand, and

43464

nothing can in the very slightest degree alter that dread writing. Hence the hopeless inaction and despairing resignation which has so long brooded over Muḥammadan lands. Buddha's teaching about *Karma* was in a measure very different from this, since Karma (" deed ") denotes the sum total of all a man's doings, good and bad, in all his many lives, and is not fixed by any Divine decree. None the less the past is unchangeable, and the future, in this and in every life, is its direct and necessary consequence. The doctrine of Necessity, so common of old in Europe, was revived and generally accepted in England in the eighteenth century, when belief in Christianity was at a low ebb. Something of the kind seems inseparable from any view of the Universe but the Christian.

In China, too, this is exemplified in the philosophy of Laou-tsze, the founder of Taouism. He taught,[1] like Buddha, that repose and inactivity far transcend in value the virtue of action.

For man now and every living thing, the best hope is not to die, the best gain not to be born, not to live. There is nothing real ; also nothing to be called unreal, " not is." Man knows not the cause of his life or death. Both are subject to mere fate. Life is a dream ; and when it ends, this is because the time has come. Death comes ; and why ? Because its time, too, has come. Rejoice not, then, in life, and mourn not in death. Now since I am here, a man on the red earth, and it is hard to escape from the body, the best thing is to seek for a mountain or riverside of renown, and invoke the pure air of heaven and earth, and the light of the sun and moon, sitting in a straw hovel, and so wait for the change and dissolution of body and heart, the " very cuffs of the sleeves of your thoughts " being unpolluted by earth. If this will not do, then in far travel seek for some secluded valley for

---

[1] Vide Archdeacon Moule's *The Splendour of a Great Hope,* pp. 102–104.

repose. . . . This world of ours is a great, confused and chaotic
world. The past, the present, are a confused past and present.
. . . Let man return to " do nothing," and it will be well with
him.

So much for past and present, according to non-
Christian views. But what about the distant future, the
result of all man's toil, sorrow, suffering ? What is man
to look forward to at last on earth ? Will life prevail,
or death, good or evil, sorrow or joy ?

It has often been pointed out that in this matter again
there is a great distinction between the Christian faith
and most non-Christian religions. With a few exceptions, to be considered later, other religions look *back* to
a lost and irrecoverable Golden Age. We find this idea
in one form or another in both the Old World and the
New, among Âryans, Semites, Bantus, and in fact among
at least some branches of each of the great families of
mankind. Christianity, however (though the Bible tells
us of a time when man was sinless, and shows how he
fell through choosing his own will rather than God's)
points forward to a yet more glorious future. Other
faiths agree in holding traditions of a happy past, but
are generally either devoid of any future hope for the
world or are at least—with such noteworthy exceptions
as those to which we have referred—very vague in their
anticipations. There was not hope enough to lighten
the gloom. As Sir William Ramsay has said :—

The practically universal view in the ancient world was that
decay and degeneration were the law of the world ; that the Golden
Age lay in the beginning, and every subsequent period was a step
further down from the primitive period of goodness, happiness,
and sympathy with the Divine Nature. We are too apt to pooh-
pooh this ancient doctrine as merely an old fashion, springing from
the natural tendency of mankind to praise the former times and
ways. But it was much more than this. It was the reasoned

view of the philosophers. It coloured almost all Greek and Roman literature. It lay deep in the heart of the pagan world. It produced the tone of sadness which is hardly ever absent from the poetry of Greece and Rome, heard as an occasional note even in its poems of pleasure.[1]

The Greek tradition of the four ages, the Golden, the Silver, the Bronze and the Iron, in the last of which men of their own age lived, is given by Hesiod [2] and by Ovid,[3] and is too well known to need remark. There is a very faint indication that Hesiod looked forward to the fifth [4] or coming age as in some way better, but he does not tell us how. Vergil's pseudo-prophecy [5] of the time when the Golden Age would return can hardly represent the heathen view on this subject : it is much more usually and probably thought to have been derived from Isaiah. The Hindû account [6] of the four ages (yugas), the Satya (or Kṛita), the Treta, the Dvâpara, and the Kali, resembles the Classical, but knows nothing of a future age of bliss for the world, since at the end of the fourth age everything is to be destroyed : unless we consider that the ceaseless recurrence of such ages is a happy prospect.

The ancient Egyptians, too, though not knowing anything of the four Ages, yet held that the past was bright and the future dark. "Certain expressions used by Egyptian writers," says Maspero,[7] "are in themselves sufficient to show that the first generations of men were

[1] *Contemporary Review.*
[2] *Works and Days*, vv. 109–201.
[3] *Metamorph*, Lib. I., vv. 89–150.
[4] *Works and Days*, vv. 174, 175.
[5] Fourth Eclogue.
[6] Manu, Dharmaśâstra, i., 79, *sqq* : Vishṇu-Purâṇa, vi., Aitar. Brâhm. ; Muṇḍ. Upan., etc.
[7] *Dawn of Civilization*, p. 158, note 3.

supposed to have lived in a state of happiness and perfection. To the Egyptians ' the times of Rā',' ' the times of the god,'—that is to say the centuries immediately following on the creation—were the ideal age, and no good thing had appeared upon earth since then." In the religions of many other peoples also, ancient and modern, we find the tradition of a Fall [1] and the belief that man's original condition was far better than the present, not only and not even principally in material prosperity and comfort, in immunity from sickness, old age and death, but especially in nearness to God and freedom from moral evil. Thus many heathen religions held with regard to the race what Wordsworth states of the individuals who compose it,

> Heaven lies about us in our infancy.

Few of them, however, saw any hope for either the race or the individual in the present or the future on earth.

But Christianity is the Religion of Hope, as well as of Faith and of Love. In Christianity Hope cannot die, though in the bright future it is to be lost in sight, in realization. Meanwhile to the Christian " to live is Christ." He is not called upon to renounce action but to be a fellow-worker with God, knowing that his " labour is not in vain in the Lord." He believes not in a blind, relentless fate, but in a Heavenly Father, the Living God, Who careth for all, without Whom not even a sparrow can fall to the ground, Who makes all things work to-

---

[1] Thus in Yasna, Hy. 9, Haoma tells Zoroaster that " The first of mortals to whom I manifested myself was Vivañvat, father of Yima, under whom flourished the blessed age which knew not cold of winter or scorching heat of summer, old age or death, or Daêva-produced hatred." The story of Yima's fall is given in Yasht xix.

gether for good to those who love Him because He first loved them. The Christian is taught that God is working out His " purpose of the Ages," [1] and that in very truth there does exist in His mind a

> Far-off Divine event
> To which the whole creation moves.

Hence he knows, too,

> That nothing walks with aimless feet ;
>   That not one life shall be destroyed,
>   Or cast as rubbish to the void,
> When God hath made the pile complete.

In this matter, as in all others, the Christian faith preserves all that is good and true in human traditions, speculations and intuitions, at the same time eliminating all that is vague, imperfect and unworthy, giving certainty for doubt, hope for despair, authority in place of conjecture, and the vision of a bright future instead of a retrospect full of vain regret and an aching sense of irretrievable loss.

[1] Eph. iii. 11.

CHAPTER IX

The Final Triumph of Life and of Good

BELIEF in an age-long contest between life and death, good and evil, is found in some form in many religions. Occasionally this tenet occurs in the guise of a tradition that at some time the whole visible universe will be destroyed, and apparently death will triumph. In another form we find it stated that this destruction will not be final, because it will be followed by a renovation of the world. Even in those faiths in which no such renewal can now be traced, it may still have been believed; or this part of a very ancient tradition may have been forgotten or rejected by the holders of that particular religion. Both tenets—that of the coming destruction of the world and that of its subsequent restoration—are of manifest interest to the student of Comparative Religion, none the less so because both are taught clearly and unmistakably in the Holy Scriptures.

In ancient Egypt, as Plato implies [1] in his account of Solon's visit to that country and his conversation with its wise men (who held the Greeks to be but children in antiquity and in knowledge), there was a theory that the world had already several times been destroyed by flood or fire, and renewed after every such catastrophe. The account of one such cataclysm is given in an in-

[1] In the *Timaeus*.

scription in the tomb of Seti I.   It is a fair inference that
the Egyptians thought that the process of destruction
and renovation would continue in the future.   In any
case the theory of the repetition of such occurrences in
the past reminds us very much of the Indian view.   The
Mahâbhârata and many other Sanskṛit works testify to
the fact that the belief was widespread that, at the end
of the present age (the *Kali-yuga*), the universe would be
destroyed.   This catastrophe is to be caused by a great
conflagration (*pralaya-dahana*), aided by a violent storm
of wind bursting forth from a dark cloud (*pralaya-ghana*),
in which will be heard the loud rumbling of thunder
(*pralaya-jala-dhara-dhvâna*).   Kalki, the final Avatâra of
Vishṇu, will then appear, mounted on a white horse,
bearing in his hand a drawn sword, with which he will
destroy evil men.   It is possible that this last detail has
been borrowed from the Bible,[1] but the fact of the approaching destruction of the world by fire must have been
a genuine Indian tenet in ancient times, for it is mentioned in the sacred books of the Buddhists of Ceylon
also, and in both Hindû and Buddhist belief such an
event is only one of a series.   The *Tipiṭakas,* or books of
the Southern Buddhist Canon, say that each of the great
worlds (*chakkavaḷas*) is subject, and will to all eternity
be subject, to an incessant process of alternately recurring
destruction and renovation.   This destruction is produced by fire, water, or wind, by which the world is either
resolved into its elements or entirely consumed.   When
this has taken place, after a long period the process of
renovation begins, and it is gradually completed, only
to be followed after a long delay by another destruction
of all things.   This process, however, is aimless and leads

[1] Cf. Rev. vi. 8, but see p. 115.

to no result, for death and life triumph over one another alternately to all eternity. In Indian belief also the four ages to which reference has already been made, as together forming an immense period of time called a Mahâ-yuga, follow one another unceasingly in regular order, the fourth age always ending in the destruction of the universe, which perishes only to come into existence again and again, quite aimlessly. The recurrence of this process of annihilation and renewal, however, may fairly be considered to be merely a philosophical development of the earlier and simpler view that the world would be destroyed and would then be finally restored to its original state of perfection. For in Persia, Greece, Rome, and Scandinavia, in which something of this view is found, no such ever-recurring cycle occurs.

Some would explain the resemblance between Egyptian, Indian and European myths of this kind to the influence which Babylonia is supposed to have exercised in very early times over " Egypt and ancient Arabia, and 'therefore Elam, Îrân, Persia, India, China, together with the pre-Greek ' Mycenaean ' civilization, the Etruscan, and the ancient American." [1] A simpler theory would be to hold that the resemblance is due to the fact that men carried with them [2] from their original home in the plain of Shinar,[3] in lower Babylonia, traditions regarding past events, and information concerning the future, which had been vouchsafed to their ancestors. This will account for differences in detail as well as for such resemblances as occur. It has the additional advantage of removing

[1] Alf. Jeremias, *The Old Testament in the Light of the Ancient East*, vol. i., cap. i.
[2] See this more fully dealt with in ch. xvi.
[3] Gen. xi. 2.

the difficulty involved in the supposition that, at any period after the separation of the nations from one another, they were ready and eager to accept a system of teaching (" founded, it would seem, upon a purely astro-nomical theory "), spread among them by Babylonian teachers, who must have gone forth from that one centre to the extreme limits of the world to propagate their views, and must have been wonderfully successful in doing so, as far as principles are concerned, though appar-ently quite careless of almost every variety in details. Strangely enough, too, their great mission has left no trace in history.

From Cicero, Juvenal, Lucretius, Propertius and others, we learn that the Romans [1] agreed with the Hindûs in holding that a time would come when the earth and the sky would be burnt up.   The myth of Phaëthon, which relates how the latter very nearly caused the premature occurrence of the catastrophe by mismanaging the fiery steeds yoked to the chariot of his father the Sun-god, shows that the Greeks, too, had a tradition to the same effect.   It was doubtless from this popular belief that the Stoics borrowed the essence of their dogma on the subject.   They taught that the stars were fiery masses, the flames of which were fed by the vapours drawn up by the sun from land and sea.   As " the flame of the Æther and the fire of the stars " consume this vapour, so, they held, the world itself would also at last be con-sumed.   Yet it is worthy of note that they, too, taught that from amid the fire the world would spring up new and fresh through the power of God.[2]

---

[1] Cic., *De Divinatione*, i., 49 ; Propertius, iii., 5, 31 ;   Juvenal, xiii., 226 ; Lucretius, v., 381 *sqq.*

[2] Balbus the Stoic, in Cicero, *De Nat. Deor.*, ii., 46.

This latter idea is very remarkable, the more so because it is found in a fully developed form in two great religious systems belonging to different nations of the Âryan family, the Persian Zoroastrians on the one hand and the Scandinavians on the other.

The Zoroastrians do not seem to have interested themselves much in the matter of the destruction of the present world,[1] but they were deeply concerned with the question how the long-continued struggle between light and darkness, life and death, good and evil, was to end. They unquestionably believed that Ahura Mazdâ (Ôrmazd) would finally triumph over Añrô Mainyuš (Ahriman), and that the world would then be renewed and restored to its original condition of goodness and happiness, all the creatures of the Evil Principle having been destroyed. This must have been part of the original teaching of Zoroaster (about 660 B.C.), if the Gâthâs are his composition, as seems to be very generally supposed, for the doctrine pervades these hymns. Somewhat later we are told that at the time of the end " Saoshyañs the Victorious and his assistants "[2] will make " a fresh world, not growing old, undying, undecaying, incorruptible, ever-living, ever beneficent," and that in it " the departed " will " rise again," that immortal life will come, freshness be given, at Saoshyañs' will. Saoshyañs and his three comrades will, during a long period of years, prepare the world for the " renovation " or " restoration " (frashô-kereti) which is ultimately to crown Ôrmazd's triumph and that of right over the Evil Principle

---

[1] Unless we take the story of the fearfully severe winter of Mahrkûsha, foretold to Yima, as representing the Iranian opinion about this, as it probably did.

[2] Yasht xix., §§ 88, 89.

and his creatures, darkness, disease and death. It is
true that this teaching, at earliest, can hardly be traced
back to as early a period as that of the settlement of
Israelite captives in " the cities [1] of the Medes " (2 Kings
xvii. 6, and xviii. 11) about 734 and 721 B.C.   Nor does
the doctrine of the resurrection of the body occur in the
Gâthâs, though it does later in Yasht xix. in the passage
we have quoted. Very possibly it was derived from
Israel,[2] though this question can hardly be definitely
settled.   At any rate its occurrence is well worthy of note.
If the idea of Saoshyañs is not borrowed from the Messianic prophecies but is an ancient Âryan tradition, we
must trace in it a very precious survival of a primeval
revelation.[3]

Much difference of opinion exists as to the date of the
various parts of the Avesta which are still preserved. But,
without going into this, we must here point out that Plutarch's reference [4] to the Persian doctrine of a long struggle between Ôrmazd and Ahriman shows that this belief
was prevalent, and had long been so, among Zoroaster's
disciples at the time when the distinguished Bœotian
wrote (A.D. 80). A later and much fuller account of the
Zoroastrian doctrine on the subject of the origin and the
predicted issue of this contest is contained in the Pahlavî
book entitled *Bûndahishnîh* or " Creation." It is true

---

[1] Another reading is " mountains."

[2] It has been said that these idolatrous and polytheistic captives
would not be likely to carry religious truth with them.   Yet some
among them " had not bowed the knee to Baal," doubtless, just
as in Elijah's time true religion lingered in some hearts.   Trouble
would lead such people to turn to God and to teach others around
them what they knew, as occurred in Babylon later.

[3] Cf. Gen. iii. 15.

[4] *De Iside et Osiride*, cap. xlix.

I

that De Harlez holds that this book in its present form
" probably dates from the epoch of the Sâsânides (A.D.
218–640), but was finished or completed after the Arabian
conquest "[1] of Persia.   Yet the work is in some measure
based upon older books which are no longer extant, and
therefore it doubtless contains ancient beliefs, somewhat
modified perhaps by outside influences, or intermixed
with more modern glosses. The following passage is
instructive as showing to what it was held the predicted
victory of good over evil would be due [2]:—

" Concerning this matter the Evil Spirit reflected,
[deeming] that Ôrmazd had fallen into a state of feeble-
ness, and that he had on that account proposed peace :
and he accepted it not.   Accordingly they went to war.
Thereupon Ôrmazd said, ' Thou art not omniscient and
omnipotent, Evil Spirit, for thou canst not kill me ; therefore, thou canst not so deal with my creation that it shall
not again return to my possession.'   Then through his
omniscience Ôrmazd knew, ' If I do not fix a time for
the contest, then he will be able to torment my creation ;
he can make them his own, even as now also men are in
a great state of admixture [of good and evil], since they
do more wrong than right.'   Therefore, Ôrmazd said to
the Evil Spirit, ' I appoint for the conflict a period of 9,000
years, in admixture [of good and evil].'   For he knew
that in that space of time he would render the Evil Spirit
powerless.   Then through blindness and ignorance the
Evil Spirit agreed to that treaty.   They resembled two
warriors who fix a time, saying, ' I fix a certain day for
the contest.'   It was Ôrmazd who through his omniscience knew that, of these 9,000 years, 3,000 would pass

[1] *Manuel de la langue pehlvie*, p. 85.
[2] *Bûndahishnîh*, §§ 3–5.

according to Ôrmazd's will, 3,000 years in an admixture
of the will of Ôrmazd and Ahriman, and finally for 3,000
years the Evil Spirit would be powerless, he would be
restrained from effecting any opposition. Then Ôrmazd repeated the *Ahuna Vairya*,[1] he pronounced ' *Yathâ
Ahû Vairyô* with its twenty-one words. He then declared
to the Evil Spirit the [certainty of the] accomplishment
of his own victory, the defeat of the Evil Spirit, the destruction of the demons, the resurrection of the final (i.e.,
future) body, the creatures' release from opposition for
ever and ever. And, because he perceived his own defeat
and the destruction of the demons, the Evil Spirit became
disheartened ; he fell back into thick darkness. Accordingly it is stated in the Law that when one-third of it had
been told him, the Evil Spirit through fear became bent
in body ; when two parts had been told, he fell on his
knee ; and, when it had all been told, he became disheartened and powerless to do harm to Ôrmazd's creation. He remained in dejection for 3,000 years. During
Ahriman's dejection Ôrmazd made the creation. He
first produced Vôhumanô (Bahman), who was [the cause
of] the prosperity of Ôrmazd's creation."

We have already seen [2] that the work of the " renovation " of the world was to be finally accomplished
through three prophets descended from Zoroaster himself. Of these the last and chief will be Saoshyañs, also
called Astvaṭ-ereta, who, 3,000 years after Zoroaster,
will appear from Lake Kāsavî, as a messenger of Ahura-
Mazdâ.[3] His coadjutors, Ukhshyaṭ-ereta and Ukhshyaṭ-

---

[1] A famous Zoroastrian prayer or charm, supposed to possess
magical power. It begins with the words, *Yathâ Ahû Vairyô*.
See p. 189.

[2] P. 95.

[3] Yasht xix., §§ 89–92.

nemañh, were to appear before his coming at intervals and in different regions, a thousand years elapsing between the birth of each of the three. Ahriman's creatures are to be destroyed, but no such terrible catastrophe [1] is mentioned as that spoken of in the Scandinavian tradition which we now proceed to detail.

Both the Older [2] and the Younger [3] Edda tell us how the world is to end, and what will follow Ragnarök, " the Twilight of the Gods." This is to be ushered in by a terribly severe winter called Fimbul-vetr. " Then shall snow drive from all directions, then shall there be great frosts and violent winds : of the sun shall there be no enjoyment. Those winters go three together, and no summer between." Three other similar winters follow ; then shall come a time of many battles and much bloodshed. " Then shall brothers slay one another for the

---

[1] It must be noticed, however, that in the *Dâthistân i Dênîk* (xxxvii., 94, 95) it is said that, after the destruction of almost all living beings in the frost and snow of the " Winter of Malkôsh (Mahrkûsha)," the world is to be repeopled by those men, animals and plants which will be preserved (Vendidad ii, 21–43), in Yima's " Vara " (enclosure), and that these " new men are substituted for the former created beings, *which is an upraising of the dead*." Does this mean that the " resurrection of the dead " was to be regarded as merely figurative, and that no such thing would actually occur ? If so, the resemblance between the Zoroastrian and the Scandinavian view as to the repeopling of the world is remarkable, and this resemblance increases the probability that such is the real meaning of the Avestic teaching on the subject. That the story of Yima's *Vara* does not refer to the Flood, but to some event which the writers of the Vendidad regarded as still future, is shown by the Pârsî chronology which, dating Yima's accession at 3,347 B.C. (according to West), makes the winter of Mahrkûsha begin A.D. 770.

[2] *Völuspá*, and *Valfth.*, vv. 18–51.

[3] *Gylfaginning*, capp. li., *fin.*

sake of greed, and in murder or breach of kinship one
shall spare neither father nor son." There shall be

> A battle-age, a sword-age,
> Shields cleft,
> A wind-age, a wolf-age,
> Ere man's-age perish.[1]

A wolf shall swallow the sun, another the moon.
" Then shall the stars vanish from the sky. Then, too,
shall it come to pass that the whole earth and the mountains shall so tremble that trees shall be rent up from the
earth, and the mountains shall be shattered." The
terrible Fenris-wolf breaks his bonds, and the great Midhgardhsorm, the Snake that surrounds the earth (i.e., the
ocean), is stirred up by the wrath of the giants, the foes
of the gods. It sweeps over the land, bearing on its
bosom Naglfar, the dread Bark of the dead, made of dead
men's nails. The lower jaw of the Fenris-wolf rests on
the earth, the upper touches the sky : from eyes and
nostrils dart forth flames. With fearful din does the
ocean's foam burst over the earth ; it even fills the air.
Amid the raging of the elements the sky cleaves asunder,
and forth from it ride Muspell's sons, the Fire-giants of
the Equatorial Zone. " Surt[2] rides in front, and before
him and behind him fire burns. Very good is his sword ;
it shines brighter than the sun. And when they ride
over Bifröst ['the trembling way,' i.e. the rainbow],
then it breaks."

To the battlefield of Vígrídh press forward Muspell's
sons. Thither, too, come the Fenris-wolf, Midhgardhsorm,
the Evil Principle Loki, Hrym and all the Frost-giants.
All the Goddess Hel's companions follow her father Loki.

---

[1] *Vóluspá*, v. 46.　　[2] Cf. p. 107.

Then Heimdall, one of the twelve Æsir or supreme Gods, sons of Ódhin, stands up and quickly blows his mighty horn to arouse the Gods to council. " Then trembles the ashtree of Yggdrasill, nor is there then in heaven or earth aught free from dread. The Æsir and all the Champions (*einherjar*) array themselves and press forward to the battlefield. Ódhin rides first, with golden helm and bright breastplate and his javelin." Fierce hand-to-hand single combats take place, in which it often happens that both of the opponents fall, each slain by the other. Thór kills Midhgardhsorm, but himself falls dead from the venom poured forth upon him by the dying monster. The wolf swallows Ódhin, but is then rent asunder by Vidhar, one of the latter's sons. " Thereupon Surt hurls fire over the earth and burns up all the world."

> The Sun shall grow black,
> Earth sinks into the sea :
> From heaven shall vanish
> The bright stars :
> Smoke rages
> And flame,
> The high heat plays
> Upon heaven itself.[1]

Of the whole human race only two members will survive, a woman name Líf (" life ") and her husband Lífthrasir (" struggle for life "). They will hide themselves in Hoddmímir's Wood during Ragnarök, " and they will have the morning dewdrops for meat : and from these persons shall come so numerous a progeny that the whole world will be populated." All the gods perish except Vidhar and his brother Vali, who live uninjured by flood or flame. From the ocean the earth rises once

[1] *Völuspá*, v. 59.

more, as the Vala (prophetess) says, for in her vision of
the future—

> She sees arise
> A second time
> Earth from ocean
> Grandly green. . . .
> Unsown shall
> The fields grow,
> All evil be amended.[1]

Vidhar and Vali dwell in Idhavöll, where Ásgardh,
"the court of the Gods," formerly stood. Thór's sons
Módhi and Magni there join them, bringing Thór's famous
hammer. From the abode of the goddess Hel come
Baldr and his blind brother Hödhr. They all seat themselves in peace and " converse together, and they remind
each other of their runes, and talk about the events which
occurred before, about Midhgardhsorm and about the
Fenris-wolf. Then are found there in the grass those
golden tablets [2] which the gods had owned."

The goddess of the Sun had borne a daughter, Álfröd-
hull (" Redness of the Elves," a poetic title of the sun),
before being swallowed up by the wolf. The daughter
performs in the renewed world the task formerly assigned
to the mother.

> That maid shall ride,
> When the gods die,
> Her mother's paths.[3]

The dead dwell in various abodes, of which some are
happy and others full of woe. The best of them all is
that which is thus described by the Vala :—

---

[1] *Völuspá*, vv. 61, 64.

[2] Cf. the Babylonian *Tablets of Destiny*, which En Lil took from
Ti'âmat.　　　　　　　　　　　　　　[3] *Vafthr.*, v. 47.

A hall sees she stand
Fairer than the Sun,
Thatched with gold,
In Gimlé (= Gem-lea).
There shall righteous
Peoples dwell,
And for ever
Happiness enjoy.[1]

It is interesting and important to observe that both the Zoroastrians and the ancient Scandinavians, more perhaps than any other nations known to us, entertained the conviction that life is finally to prevail over death, right over wrong, light over darkness.   They could therefore more readily than others accept and welcome the Christian teaching, " We . . . look for new heavens and a new earth, wherein dwelleth righteousness."   But even among the savage inhabitants of the Andaman Islands it is held that at last the spirits of all men, good and bad alike, will be re-united with their revived bodies.   Then on a renewed earth they will live for ever, healthy and strong, never growing old, free from disease and death.

It is proverbially difficult to prove an universal negative, and so we cannot say, regarding this tenet of the final " restoration of all things "[2] and the triumph of life over death even in this earth of ours, that it has not been held far more widely than we have as yet traced it. But it is certainly safe to state that most religions do not seem to have retained this tenet.   For the most part all that we find in them is belief in an After-life, in which some or all men shall live again.   With this we proceed to deal in the next chapter.   But we must here remind our readers how both in the Old Testament and the New we find it taught, with increasing clearness, that even on

---

[1] *Völuspá*, v. 66.   [2] Ἀποκατάστασις, Acts iii. 21.

this earth life is finally to triumph over death, truth over
falsehood, right over wrong. Thus in Isaiah xi., in connexion with the coming forth of " a shoot out of the
stock of Jesse," who " with righteousness shall judge the
poor, and reprove with equity for the meek of the earth :
and He shall smite the earth with the rod of His mouth,
and with the breath of His lips shall He slay the wicked,"
we are told that " The wolf shall dwell with the lamb,
the leopard shall lie down with the kid, and the calf
and the young lion and the fatling together ; and a little
child shall lead them. . . . They shall not hurt nor
destroy in all My holy mountain : for the earth shall be
full of the knowledge of the LORD, as the waters cover
the sea." Elsewhere in the same book [1] we read : " Thy
dead shall live ; my dead bodies shall arise. Awake and
sing, ye that dwell in the dust : for thy dew is as the dew
of herbs, and the earth shall cast forth the dead." In Job
also we have the grand passage,

> I know that my Redeemer liveth,
> And that He shall stand up at the last upon the earth :
> And after my skin hath been thus destroyed,
> Yet from my flesh shall I see God.[2]

In Daniel [3] the angel says, " Many of them that sleep
in the dust of the earth shall awake, some to everlasting
life, and some to shame and everlasting contempt. And
they that be wise shall shine as the brightness of the
firmament ; and they that turn many to righteousness
as the stars for ever and ever." In the New Testament
the same doctrine is taught, but infinitely more clearly
and fully. Thus our Lord [4] speaks of " the regenera-

---

[1] Isa. xxvi. 19.
[2] Job xix. 25, 26.
[3] Dan. xii. 2, 3.
[4] Matt. xix. 28.

tion when the Son of Man shall [sit on the throne of His glory " ; and Peter reminds us that " We look for new heavens and a new earth, wherein dwelleth righteousness." [1]   Finally, in the Book of Revelation, John " saw a new heaven and a new earth : for the first heaven and the first earth are passed away ; and the sea is no more. . . .   And I heard a great voice out of the throne saying, ' Behold, the tabernacle of God is with men, and He shall dwell with them, and be their God : and He shall wipe away every tear from their eyes ; and death shall be no more, neither shall there be mourning nor crying nor pain any more : the first things are passed away.' And He that sitteth on the throne said, ' Behold, I make all things new.' " [2]   It is unnecessary to quote passages to prove from the Scriptures the Christian doctrine of the resurrection of the dead, but people often forget that the Bible teaches [3] that " the Creation itself also shall be delivered from the bondage of corruption," after " the day of the Lord," " in the which the heavens shall pass away with a great noise, and the elements shall be dissolved with fervent heat, and the earth and the works that are therein shall be burned up. [4] "

Here the question forces itself upon our attention. If certain ethnic religions agree with Christianity in teaching the fiery end [5] of the world and its renewal, how are we to account for this agreement ?   Have these religions borrowed from Christianity, or has Christianity borrowed this from them, or have both derived this teaching from a common source ?   This question de-

---

[1] 2 Pet. iii. 13 ; cf. Isa. lxv. 17.   [2] Rev. xxi. 1, 3–5.
[3] Rom. viii. 21.   [4] 2 Pet. iii. 10.
[5] Cf. Lucan, *Pharsalia*, Lib. VII., 812–815 ; Ovid, *Metam.*, Lib. i. 256 *sqq.* ; Prose Edda, " Beguiling of Gylfi," cap. iv., *fin.*, etc.

mands an answer, but not perhaps by itself and in connexion with this one tenet alone : for it is part of the
great question of the relation between Christianity and
the ethnic faiths in general.   As we proceed in our investigation into religions, we shall see that in nearly every
section of the subject this comparison between Christianity and other religions forces itself upon our notice,
though nowhere perhaps more clearly than here.   The
natural place for dealing with it therefore will be our
concluding chapter.

CHAPTER X

The After-Life

" THE consideration of eternity," as has well been said,[1] " is the true sanction of morals, because it is that consideration which alone makes anything of any consequence. It imparts the one real and enduring vital import. It has been sometimes said that this is a mean view, but life itself is meanness apart from the motive of eternity."

All nations of men have at all times felt this in some measure. The religious ideas of different tribes and faiths nowhere perhaps vary from one another more than concerning the After-life; yet it is not too much to say that all nations and all religions agree in holding that death does not end all, that for many men at least, if not for all men, there is an existence after death. Regarding the nature of that existence, its duration, its happiness or misery, its employments and other details, the differences of view are almost innumerable; but this renders it all the more remarkable that there should be general agreement upon the fact that there is a future life. This may perhaps support the view that, whereas the differences may be due to man's ignorance and his attempts to make imagination supply the place of infor-

[1] Waite, *Introduction to Obermann*.

mation, the agreement rests upon some very solid basis. Whether, however, this conviction that life survives death be due to instinct, to experience, to tradition, to an early revelation, or to some evolution of thought, does not now concern us : it suffices for us that the fact of such a belief is beyond dispute.

Among many peoples we find the idea that man was not originally subject to death, as he evidently now is ; that death came upon the human race from outside, so to speak, and might have been avoided. The *Rig-Veda* leads us to understand that Yama, the first man who died, and who became the ruler of the realms of the dead, need not have died had he not committed some offence. Hesiod speaks of death coming upon the first race of men, but as gently as sleep. Many savage tribes still believe that death is so unnatural that, if a member of the tribe die, then clearly he must have been bewitched or poisoned. The ancient Babylonians, though they regarded man as originally mortal, yet held that Adapa, the first man, was by Anu offered heavenly food which would have rendered him immortal. By refusing it he condemned himself and his posterity to death. On the other hand, among the many contradictions of Hindûism is the declaration that even the gods (*devas*) were at first liable to death, and that they became immortal only through performing certain religious rites. Thus the Śatapatha-brâhmaṇa says :—

> The gods lived constantly in dread of Death—
> The mighty Ender (*Antaka*)—so with toilsome rites
> They worshipped and repeated sacrifices
> Till they became immortal. Then the Ender
> Said to the gods, " As ye have made yourselves
> Imperishable, so will men endeavour

> To free themselves from me ; what portion then
> Shall I possess in man ? " The gods replied,
> " Henceforth no being shall become immortal
> In his own body ; this his mortal frame
> Shalt thou still seize ; this shall remain thy own.
> He who through knowledge or religious acts
> Henceforth attains to immortality
> Shall first present his body, Death, to thee." [1]

The Avesta teaches us that death, disease and suffering are all creatures of the Evil Principle, and were by him brought into existence *after* the Good Principle had produced all good things. Here again death was not held to be natural but unnatural. Neither fire nor air nor water would produce death, since these were all good creatures of Ahura Mazdâ : those who seemed to die by drowning or to be burnt alive were in reality slain by some evil spirit created by Añrô-Mainyuš.

When we come to consider the various opinions which have been entertained regarding the nature of the existence after death, we find very great divergence. The Babylonian description of the abode of the dead given in the legend of the Descent of Ishtar very fairly reveals the general view of the Semites on the subject, apart from revelation. It is called " the Land of No Return, . . . the house of gloom, the dwelling of Irkalla, the house from which those who enter depart not, the road from whose path there is no return ; the house where they who enter are deprived of light, a place where dust is their nourishment, clay their food : the light they behold not, in thick darkness they dwell ; they are clad like bats in a garb of wings, on door and bolt the dust is laid." [2] That this was the general Semitic opinion about the abode

---

[1] Monier Williams, *Hindûism*, pp. 35, 36.
[2] Sayce, *Religions of Egypt and Babylonia*, p. 427.

of the dead is confirmed by Job's account of the belief
which he and his people in the Land of Uz entertained
on the same subject :—

> Let me alone, that I may take comfort a little,
> Before I go whence I shall not return,
> Even to the land of darkness and of the shadow of death ;
> A land of thick darkness, as darkness itself ;
> A land of the shadow of death, without any order,
> And where the light is as darkness.[1]

Such was the Sheol where men " were gathered unto
their fathers," where there does not seem to have been
any happiness expected, except the negative happiness
of being where " the wicked cease from troubling, and
the weary are at rest." [2]

When we turn to Ancient Egypt, we find a certain
amount of difference in the view taken of existence in
the next world. It is well known that the *Book of the
Dead* is filled with details of the perils encountered by
the human spirit after its departure from the body,
while journeying to the " Fields of Reeds," and of its
occupations there and in other parts of the " Fields of
Peace " (*Sekhetu Ḥetep*). But before this, soon after
death, the heart (or conscience) of the deceased is weighed
in Osiris' presence against the statue or symbol of Ma'āt
or Truth. If it proves too light, it is devoured by a
monster termed the " Eater of the Dead," which fact
probably denoted belief in the annihilation of the wicked.
The " justified " man lived in a happiness similar to
that men experience in the present world, in the enjoyment of eating, drinking, hunting and other carnal
delights. He met and recognized his dead relatives.
Slaves worked in the field for him. Originally, no doubt,

[1] Job x. 20–22.   [2] Job iii. 17.

his servants had been slain and buried with the great man ; but in later times they were represented by small clay figures (*ushebtiu*) laid with the mummy in the tomb. The worshipper of Osiris held that his salvation depended upon his abstinence in this earthly life from gross sins, and he had therefore a lofty code of morality. His happiness in the world to come arose from his union with Osiris, the " Chief of the Underworld." It seems very doubtful whether the Egyptians believed in a resurrection of the body. They appear rather to have fancied that a kind of spiritual body (*sā'ḫu*) was gradually developed from the mummified material body, and that it clothed the spiritual part of the man. But this religion of Osiris was only one form of the composite religion of the Egyptians, though it was older and nobler than that of Rā', the Sun-god, which in later times partly supplanted it. The devotee of Rā' held that after death only the special favourites of this god were finally absorbed into him and thus continued, though with loss of personality, to travel in his chariot through the sky. The rest of the saved were set in the Underworld to cultivate their fields in darkness, except while the Sun's bark gave them light in passing. Salvation depended on the knowledge of a mass of sacred formulae, the moral element to be found in the Osirian creed having vanished. The lost suffered ages of agonizing torture, and most of the rest spent their time in gloomy shade. Thus, in Egypt too we find the belief held that

> The Underworld is a land of thick darkness,
> A sorrowful place for the dead. [1]

In the Egyptian psychology, the part of man which

[1] Sayce, *Religions of Ancient Egypt and Babylonia*, p. 202.

survived death was not single but composite, as we find in some other nations and especially among certain savage tribes. The " double " (*ka*, or rather *ku*) or vital principle of the deceased lived generally in the tomb, eating and drinking the food provided, or else compelled to live on offal. The " soul " (*ba*, represented as a bird with a human head) could visit the body and assume various shapes. In some places it is said to ascend to heaven and dwell with Rā'. In spite of its wings the soul, at least in early days, seems to have mounted to the " iron firmament " by means of a ladder. The " luminous essence " (*khu*, afterwards in the Hermetic books identified with the mind) was the higher part of the *ba*. Besides this were the " heart " (or conscience, *àb*), the " shadow " (*khaibit*), and the " spiritual body " (*sā'ḥu*). Even among the " pre-dynastic " Egyptians, judging by their tombs, there was a firm belief in the survival of the soul after the death of the body. Indeed, many of the tenets already mentioned were probably inherited from them. It is some of the oldest texts [1] that place the world of the dead above the sky. Later ideas transferred it to the north, the north-west, or the west of Egypt, and then came to regard it as beneath the earth, in the region visited by the Sun during the night.

The ancient Greeks, like most if not all other Áryan tribes, believed in the existence of an unseen world, generally regarded as beneath the earth, where the dead dwelt in darkness. To enter it, a voyage was necessary to the land of the Kimmerioi, lying to the north apparently. Ere the spirit of a dead person could there find rest, his body must be buried or burnt, and he had to cross the river of death. Some of the greatest criminals, after

---

[1] In the Pyramid of Pepi I.

K

being judged, were condemned to the torments of Tartaros, a region far below Hades. A few favoured spirits went to the Elysian Fields in the far west. But existence after death was shadowy, less so in Elysium than elsewhere, however, because the Elysian Plains were on earth and not in the Underworld.

The idea that the life after death is very similar to the present life in many respects is found among many different tribes, ancient as well as modern. The habit of burying with the deceased, or burning upon his funeral pyre, the instruments which he used in daily life, and even his wives and slaves, existed in many lands in the most ancient times, as we learn not only from the oldest records, but also from the contents of barrows or tumuli. A good example of such belief is found in the religion of the Tartars as late as the thirteenth century of our era. With the dead man they used to bury a large supply of flesh for food, and garments ; and even the poorest supplied their deceased friend with a little money. The rich gave changes of raiment besides these things, and placed a valuable robe under the dead man's head, to be given (instead of what he wore) to any one who wished to plunder him on his journey. Great men had their horses interred with them, but each horse was first ridden to death, eviscerated, stuffed with grass,[1] impaled, and bidden to be ready whenever his lord should require. With the Khan of the tribe, however, in addition to everything else, treasures and precious stones were buried. A number of slaves, sometimes as many as twenty, were interred alive with him, to attend on him when he awoke.[2]

[1] Cf. Herodotus, Lib. IV, 72.
[2] Ricoldi, *Liber Peregrinationis*, cap. 9.

In some parts of the world it seems to be thought that the spirit lives indefinitely, if not eternally, after death ; in others that its existence is long but not eternal ; in others that the chiefs alone enjoy a continual existence, the souls of the common people gradually growing feebler in the After-life and finally ceasing to exist. Some hold that the 'spirits of men come from the sky, enter the world at birth, and return to the heaven at death. Thus the Maoris believed that the spirits of mortals first began to live in the seventh heaven : that when in their descent they reached the fourth heaven, they were there fitted for life on earth, and thence came down and were born as men. After death, the spirits of the chiefs went to dwell in the sky, but those of the other dead descended to the realm of Night (Po), where ruled the Great Girl of Night (Hine-nui-te-Po) in Reinga, a region which gave its name to the cape at the north-west of New Zealand, near which is the entrance to the abode of the dead. The spirit passes through various regions of the lower world, degenerating in each. In the ninth, Toke (" worm "), it becomes a worm, and when this worm dies, in the tenth and lowest region the spirit ceases to exist. Among the Bantus of Africa some hold that the spirit ascends to heaven or " goes home." In the *Rig-Veda* the same term, " going home," is applied to the departure of the spirit for Yama's realm as well as to the sun at his setting. In Europe, Empedocles taught that the human spirit had come from a higher world, probably agreeing therein with what was inculcated in the Orphic mysteries and held by the Pythagoreans. Apuleius attributes to Asclepius the doctrine that " a *return* to heaven " is denied to the wicked, and that they are compelled to suffer transmigration as a punishment. Pindar held that an " ancient sin " compelled the human spirit to confinement in the body for a time, and to live for three lives on earth to atone for this sin, ere finally going to the Isle of the Blest where Kronos reigns over the heroes of old.

The doctrine of the transmigration of the soul is found among the natives of Australia. It does not appear in Vedic India, but is fully developed in Manu's time. In Western Mithraism the same belief prevailed, according at least to some writers.[1] It was also prevalent among some South American tribes. The Kelts, as we are informed by classical authors, were firm believers in this doctrine, and it occurs elsewhere in many places and among many peoples.

Ancestor-worship, in some form or other, was at one time almost universal, and is still the great feature of the actual practical religion of the Chinese, and hardly less of the Japanese and Hindûs. The Chinese hold that the immaterial part of man is threefold, consisting of the *kuei*, which remains near the grave of the deceased, the *ling*, or soul proper, which is affected by the passions, and the *huen*, or " rational soul " (spirit) which during life inhabits the brain. The *huen*, when it leaves the body at death, for a time dwells in a " double " made of silk, and after the funeral takes up its permanent abode in the ancestral tablet in the funeral hall of the family, where it receives semi-divine honours. Among the ancient Romans almost the whole of the institutions of both family and State were based upon the worship paid to ancestors on the father's side. The family existed mainly to carry on perpetually the service of its ancestors, whose

[1] Ash Shahristânî says that the Mazdakians also in Persia believed in transmigration.

lot was want and misery if no son remained to show them due reverence. We are all aware that the *Manes*, the *Lares* and the *Penates*, exercised more influence upon the individual and the family than even the great gods Jupiter, Juno, Minerva, and the rest. Among the Romans also, as well as the Chinese and Egyptians, the tripartite nature of the inner man was recognized, as we learn from the verses—

> Terra teget carnem, tumulum circumvolat umbra,
> Orcus habet manes, spiritus astra petit.

But this view seems to be later than the preceding, though this is a hard matter to decide one way or the other.

It is worthy of notice that among savage tribes in many different parts of the world there still exists, as was the case in pre-dynastic Egypt, and in Europe in ancient days, the custom of placing the dead body in the tomb in the very same doubled-up position in which the child lies in his mother's womb. Doubtless this is intended to show belief in birth into another state of existence, or, as Chuang-tsze in China said about 338 B.C., " Death is the commencement of life."

In some religions no clear trace can be found of any distinction between the lot of the good and that of the bad in the After-life. Sometimes there is this distinction, sometimes instead of it there seems to be the fancy that earthly rank is continued in the next world. At other times the fate of the dead appears to be decided by some apparent accident, such as the manner or place of their death. In India at the present time, death in the waters of the Ganges, or near its banks, procures entrance to one special heaven. The Valhalla of the Norsemen was reserved for warriors slain in battle ; and Muslims hold that those who fall in a Jihâd go to Paradise at once and there dwell in the crops of green birds until the resurrection, while many at least of the other dead remain till then in Isrâfîl's trumpet, or in the well Zam-zam at Mecca, or else hover around the tomb.

Among the Aztecs of Mexico it was thought that the wicked went after death to a place of eternal darkness. Those who died of certain specified diseases dwelt in comparative ease and idleness : but men who had been sacrificed to the gods or had fallen on the battlefield went instantly to the Sun-god.   Him they accompanied on his daily course through the sky for a time ; and at last they entered a beautiful paradise, where they dwelt embodied in clouds and bright singing-birds.

In few religions but the Christian is purity of heart and life deemed necessary for entrance into eternal bliss. Often, indeed, the pleasures to be enjoyed in Paradise are depicted as carnal and material, even grossly sensual. The Muhammadan Paradise is one of the best—or worst—examples of this, with its rivers of wine, its Hourîs, its changing shapes of men and women, every indulgence being permitted in the immediate presence of God, who has provided these delights for His favourites. In Vedic times it was much the same in India.   It has well been said :—

There is very little teaching of personal purity in the Veda, and the poet who hopes for a heaven where he is to find " longing women," " desire and its fulfilment," has in mind, in all probability, purely impure delights.   It is not to be assumed that the earlier morality surpassed that of the later day, when, even in the epic, the hero's really desired heaven is one of drunkenness and women *ad libitum*.[1]

Perhaps the noblest among non-Christian views of the

[1] Hopkins, *Religions of India*, p. 148.

After-life is that contained in the Avesta. During three days after death the spirit remains near the body, guarded by the good Genius Sraosha from the assaults of the *drujes* or evil spirits. Sraosha, on the fourth day, conducts the soul to the presence of the celestial judges, Rashnu and Mithra, and then himself sits with these two assessors in judgment, holding the balance in which men's deeds are weighed. If the deceased is condemned, he falls into the darkness which is the abode and realm of the Evil Principle, Añrô-Mainyuš (Ahriman) when he tries to cross the *Chinvat-peretu* (" Bridge of the Judge ") to enter the abode of the just. The bridge is guarded by two dogs, who do not oppose the righteous crossing it. The passage is broad to the good, but too narrow for the wicked. Having passed over it, the good man enters and goes through three abodes of bliss, those of good thoughts, good words, and good works, in succession. At length he enters Garô-nmâna (in the Gâthâs styled Garô-demâna, " the Home of Song "), where Ahura-Mazdâ (Ôrmazd) dwells in light, and where the spirit of the good man is greeted by the good Genius Vôhumanô, welcomed, and congratulated on his escape from the corrupt and transitory world and entrance into eternal happiness. " How hast thou come hither to us, O righteous one, from the perishable life to the imperishable life ? "

Among the Kelts few hoped to reach the " Land of the Living " (*Tír na mBéo*), for transmigration would cause renewed life on earth. Yet certain favoured mortals might enter that happy land, where the gods dwelt, and which was sometimes said to be " under the waves," sometimes in an isle or in many islands across the sea. Many Keltic tales describe a visit to some of these blissful regions. The realm of Marzin, an Armorican god, is

thus described : " The waters, woods and meadows of
this kingdom had a beauty such that no man had ever
seen the like. All the stones were diamonds, all the
fruits and flowers had an incomparable flavour, brightness,
and scent. The inhabitants lived in games and pleasure.
They were very small, but beautifully shaped, all fair
in hue, with curls of hair on their shoulders. They rode
horses proportioned to their size, no taller than grey-
hounds. Their food consisted solely of fruits and milk ;
meat and fish disgusted them. The form of their govern-
ment was monarchical. As for religion, they did not
openly practise any ; their only worship was the love of
truth. That fair land, in which was found all that one
could wish, where people spent their time in listening to
the most delicious music, lacked but one thing, a ray of
sunlight. People lived there in perpetual twilight." [1]
These little people are the fairies of our childhood. Many
of these Keltic descriptions of Paradise represent much
of the enjoyment, however, as consisting in eating vast
quantities of pork, cooked in an inexhaustible cauldron,
and drinking gallons of ale. There was also abundance
of love-making, due to the presence of women of marvellous beauty.

Northern Buddhism, in the form in which it prevails
to-day in Tibet, China and Japan, has borrowed its idea
of an After-life from various sources, but probably in
large measure from the traditions of the Hindûs and those
of the nations among whom it is now established. It

[2] attempts to assuage the thirst for immortality, and to satisfy
the hunger for another life which torments the souls of the

---

[1] De la Villemarqué, *Myrdhinn*, p. 23.
[2] Moule, *Splendour of a Great Hope*, pp. 12, 13.

400,000,000 in these three north-eastern lands. With stolen water and secret bread Amidâbha [1] promises his followers a western heaven, where purest, sweetest, freshest water flows pellucid over golden sand, surrounded by pavements and pavilions of precious stones and jewels, with lotus flowers as large as a carriage-wheel floating on the surface, exhaling enchanting fragrance, with music of birds and harmonious voices of the winds ; and all this realm securely fenced in by sevenfold rows of trees and sevenfold nets of silk. . . . The life to come . . . shall be as this life, but much more abundant, with more money for the devout believer, more pleasure, higher honour ; then evening once again and decay and death ; or perchance you may rise to the position of genii or *lohan* ; or perchance you may sink lower, to the body of beast or bird or reptile.[2]

When philosophy arose, as in some form it did very early everywhere, it sought to test the traditions of an After-life, and to find out what evidence there was for belief in such an existence. Speaking generally, philosophy could not in the past either prove or disprove this instinctive and universal conviction. Confucius, for example, says, " while you do not know life, how can you know death ? " Tsze Kung asked him, " Do the dead have knowledge of our worship and services ? " The sage replied, " If I say Yes, filial sons and grandsons will ruin themselves in such services and offerings. If I say No, the unfilial will leave the dead unburied. There is no urgency on this point. Hereafter you will know for

[1] One of the Buddhas. His heaven is *Sukhâkara* or *Sukhâvatî*, placed in the western part of the sky.

[2] Among the Confucians there has for ages prevailed the habit of burning paper figures of various articles as part of the funeral ceremonies. This doubtless represents the ancient and widely extended custom of bestowing on the dead presents likely to be useful in the After-life.

yourself." Buddha seems to have in large measure accepted Hindû ideas regarding the After-life, or rather the great number of different existences which as a general rule must be entered upon in succession, according to the doctrine of Transmigration, even though he denied the existence in man of an ego or personality which would survive death. All existence being misery in his opinion, the goal to be aimed at was Nirvâṇa (" Extinction," first of the passions, {then of existence), and this might be attained in this life. Those who attained it, as Buddha himself is said to have done, ceased to exist at death. But belief in an After-life was so strong in Buddha that he taught that nothing but long and vigorous effort could possibly prevent men from having it. His followers, as we have seen, have largely given up the attempt, and prefer to believe in a happy existence after death.

Philosophy having failed either to prove or to disprove the After-life, what light does Christianity cast on this subject, which is of vital importance for all of us ?

Other religions, as we have seen, tell of a more or less dim and unreal After-life, or one which is all too really sensual and material in its occupations and pleasures. Generally nothing very definite is known, but in some cases hope becomes a positive belief. Not unfrequently all moral restraints are removed after death, or rewards and punishments are not thought of, or, if believed to exist, they are held to depend upon the due performance or neglect of forms and ceremonies, the repetition of charms, or even upon earthly rank. Belief in Transmigration often renders it impossible to look hopefully forward to what follows death, or even makes the thought terrible. Muḥammadan fatalism and fear of the " Torture of the Tomb," or of arbitrary condemnation, robs the prospect

of the After-life of any comfort.   Above all, in hardly
any ethnic faith is there belief in a Paradise into which
nothing that defiles can enter.   Few religions tell of a
home beyond the grave which is such as to attract a pure-
minded and spiritual, a really good, man or woman.
Even when nearness to God or the gods is promised, these
deities are not regarded—for the most part—as holy,
loving, good.   Finally, however firmly men may believe
in an After-life, they have no real *proof* of its existence
apart from Christianity.

How great a contrast the Gospel presents in this respect
to all other systems !   In the Resurrection of Christ we
have at once the *proof* of an After-life, and the evidence
that Christ's teaching regarding it is true.   When He
tells us of His Father's House of many mansions, He confirms His statement by keeping His promise to rise again.
That this actually occurred is the best-established fact in
all history, and nearly nineteen hundred centuries have
not been long enough to enable its deniers to disprove
it.   But this is not all.   His promise to be with His own
in Paradise renders the place holy and happy.   His
revelation of God is itself sufficient to make the Father's
House a Home.   " Jesus Christ hath abolished " (*or*
annulled) " death, and brought life and immortality "
(incorruption) " to light through the Gospel."   He gives
not hope but certainty, not dimness and obscurity but
the clear vision of a state in which faith is lost in sight,
and where we shall know as we are known, when we depart
and are with Christ, and grow more and more in His
image and likeness, until we reach the perfect man.   He
reveals the fact that a higher and not a lower life follows
the present, and that even Paradise is but a preparation
for the resurrection, when He shall change this body of

our humiliation that it may be like unto the body of His glory, when this corruptible shall put on incorruption and this mortal shall put on immortality, and death shall be swallowed up in victory.

CHAPTER XI

Man's Conscious Need of a Saviour

DANGER, trouble, suffering, and sorrow, to say nothing of repentance and remorse for sin, have in all ages led men to realize their need of help from some higher source. Among not a small proportion of religions, however, we find that this feeling has degenerated into the attempt to avert the enmity of wicked spirits, good ones being not unfrequently regarded as either feebler than evil ones or as too selfish to care for their petitioners. The higher religions, on the other hand, represent at least certain of the gods as benevolent and as ready to hear and answer prayer. Man needed, however, to feel persuaded of some bond of sympathy between himself and his Helper, and this natural desire led, on the one hand, to making the gods only too human in their conduct, and on the other to the development or the acceptance of belief in some form of Incarnation. This we have already seen.

Among the gods and deified men worshipped in different parts of the world there are some who in certain respects have been considered not only as Helpers but in some sense as Saviours, even though this special title has rarely, if at all, been conferred upon them.[1] Occasion-

[1] This is a matter of little importance, for one of the Ptolemies

ally these " Saviours " are real or legendary ancestors of the tribe that looks to them for help. Thus, among the aborigines of Brazil, Tamoi was said to have been the ancestor of all men, the first of men. He taught men to till the ground. He is now in the sky, and there cares for the spirits of the dead when they come thither to him. In India similarly Yama, the first man who died, was early represented as dwelling near the sun, or in the moon, and reigning over the dead.

But when we pass away from Ancestor-worship, we find, among the gods proper, and also among the great teachers of mankind, certain very prominent persons to whom especially men have looked for deliverance. Sometimes these are represented as still to come, sometimes as having lived on earth long ago and died or disappeared, and sometimes as expected to return. Thus in Mexico among the Toltecs was the tradition that a white man, whom they worshipped under the name Quetzalcoatl (" the feathered serpent "), had once lived among them as high priest at Tula. He had taught them how to serve God, and also to practise agriculture and many useful arts. At last, however, either being offended or under the influence of a magic beverage given him by the god Tetzcatlipoca, he left the country, sailing away towards the East. But he promised to return some day. This, as is well known, caused the Mexicans to fancy that the Spaniards were his children, and gave the latter the opportunity of making themselves masters of the country. It is quite possible that Quetzalcoatl was a European, conceivably a Christian missionary ; but perhaps some

---

was called *Sôtêr* (Saviour) and Nero in papyri is styled " Saviour of the World ! "

other explanation of the story may be preferred.   Reference has already [1] been made to the coming tenth *avatâra* or " descent " of Vishnu as Kalki.   The Northern Buddhists speak of a deity called Avalokita or Avalokitesvara, whom the Tibetans believe to become incarnated in the person of each successive Grand Lama.   He is really a manifestation of Šiva, and as such has many forms and a large number of limbs.   The sun and moon issue from his eyes, and rivers flow from his fingers to cool the many Buddhist hells.   All this makes him seem to be a Nature-god, and some have identified him with the sun.   His name seems to give some support to this view, as it probably means either " the contemplated (i.e. seen) lord " or " the lord of what is seen."   But in some Buddhist works he is spoken of as a Bodhisattva or future Buddha. He now dwells in Amitâbha's paradise, Sukhâvatî, and at the end of our age is to appear as the thousandth Buddha, who has promised to bring all beings into that land of bliss.   Another coming Buddha is *Maitreya* (Metteyyo), who is now in the Tusita-heaven and is the next Buddha who will be born on earth.[2]   Among the Muslims again there is the expectation of the coming Mahdî or guide, and this belief has caused many impostors to arise, and has led, in the Sûdân and elsewhere, to the shedding of oceans of blood.   We have seen,[3] too, how the Zoroastrians expected the coming of three " prophets," with an interval of a thousand years between each of them and his successor.

Turning to Northern Europe, we discover among both

---

[1] P. 107.

[2] A common form of Buddhist blessing is, " Mayest thou see Maitreya and reach Nirvâna."

[3] Pp. 95, 110–114.

Kelts and Scandinavians a belief in the future return of one whose death was deeply lamented and who is said to have been brave and good. In Wales and Brittany this person is Arthur or Lemenik, a King, while in Scandinavia it is the fair god Baldr.

The hero styled Lemenik in Brittany and Lleminawg in Wales, first owned the magic sword Excalibur, which Merlin (Merddhin) forged in the Underworld, and which afterwards passed in succession to Uthyr Penn-dragon and Arthur. Merlin is said to have prophesied that discord would reign among the Britons until Lemenik should return to unite them against their foes. Much the same prophecy is ascribed to him regarding Arthur, who, according to the *Brut Tysilio* and the *Brut G. ab Arthur*,[1] was mortally wounded in the battle of Badon (called Arderidd by the Welsh), apparently in A.D. 516. " Thence he went to the Isle of Avallach " (Apple-orchard, Glastonbury) " for healing ; and there is not here concluded more than this about Arthur's death." His compatriots fondly held that he had been taken to the Underworld for recovery and would return to deliver them from the Saxons. This deliverance was to be an earthly one only, such a deliverance as the great mass of the Jews in our Lord's time hoped that the Promised Messiah would bring them. Later still, Prince Arthur's murder by King John's order seems to have been largely due to the fact that it was well known that the Bretons and the Welsh were confident that in him Arthur had returned, and that he would give them the victory over the hated Normans. It is possible, however, that in the belief that Lemenik and Arthur would return may have lingered faint echoes

---

[1] *Myvyrian Archaiology*, pp. 472 and 546.

of some higher and more spiritual hope that once lived in the hearts of the Brythonic Kelts.

Such a hope is much clearer in the legend of Baldr as preserved in the Prose Edda.[1] He was one of Ódhin's many sons. " He is so fair in features, and so bright, that light shines forth from him. . . . He is the wisest of gods and the fairest-spoken and the mildest ; but such a disposition belongs to him that his decree may not be opposed. He dwells in the place called Breidha-blik " (broad-view) " in heaven : . . . in that place can there be nought unclean." The Edda tells us that one night Baldr dreamed a fearful dream which seemed ominous of his death. His mother Frigg took from all things but the mistletoe an oath that they would not hurt him.   The evil god Loki heard this and persuaded the blind Hödhr to throw a piece of mistletoe at Baldr, who instantly fell dead. Baldr's body was placed on the deck of his ship, together with his wife Nanna and his favourite steed, and all were consumed by fire in old Norse fashion. The gods asked Hel, daughter of Loki and goddess of the Underworld, to permit Baldr to return to earth. She agreed to this, on condition that all with one consent wept for him. One old giantess, however, refused to do so, and thus prevented him from coming back to life. Yet finally it was believed that, after the dread " Twilight of the Gods," when the " hall fairer than the sun, roofed with gold " shall stand in the Gem-meadow (*Gimlê*) for the habitation of the gods, and the world shall be renewed, then Baldr shall be there with the rest of Ódhin's family ; for we read, [2] " Fields shall grow unsown, all evil be bet-

---

[1] *Gylfaginning* ; see also *Baldrs Draumar* in the Sæmundar Edda.
[2] *Völuspá*, § 64.

tered, Baldr shall come." We are not told that he will then do anything which will be of service either to gods or men, but their love for him and pity for his early death make them both long for his deliverance from Hel's abode and restoration to life. Whether under these circumstances Baldr can in any true sense be called a " Saviour," however, is more than questionable.

Whether the unnamed child spoken of in Vergil's glorious Fourth Eclogue as about to be born to bring back the age when Saturn reigned, and to restore Justice to the earth, in any degree represents an ancient Roman tradition, we cannot say. Sir W. Ramsay says that no parallel can be found in preceding classical literature to justify us in holding that such an expectation really existed among Greeks and Romans. Hence he is of opinion that Vergil borrowed the idea, indirectly perhaps, from that wonderful prophecy in the eleventh chapter of Isaiah. But possibly some such tradition may have lingered among the Italian Âryans, for it may in a measure be compared with those we have found in India and Scandinavia as well as Persia. Doubtless the poet's intention was to flatter Pollio, whom he represents as about to become the child's father (unless that position was to belong rather to Antony or Octavianus) ; yet he was also voicing the longing for some Deliverer so widely felt at a time when things throughout the Empire, and perhaps the whole world, were at their worst. From this latter point of view this eclogue may be compared to some extent with the sixteenth epode of Horace. But we must pass on to consider some more certain and striking instances in which man's consciousness of the need of a Deliverer has expressed itself more unequivocally than in those we have mentioned as yet.

The chief god of Babylon throughout historical times was Maruduku or Marduk (the Merodach of Scripture, often styled Bêl, " the husband," " the lord "). The derivation and meaning of the god's name are still disputed, but " Marduk " is probably a contraction or corruption of the Šumerian *Amar-dugga*, " the good youth." He is often represented by the ideographs (signs for ideas) *Amar Ud*, " Youth of the Dawn," and evidently denoted the rising sun. Yet doubtless the adoration of his worshippers was directed to him as the spirit of the sun, or the god who rode in the solar chariot. The word *Amar* properly means the full-grown young of any animal. Marduk was identified with *Asari*, " the strong one," " the prince," also a solar deity. Asari was son of Ea, god of the deep, and his wife Dam-Ki-na (" lady of the earth "). Ea was frequently spoken of as *Dara-nun*, " the Ram (or Antelope) of the Heavenly Ocean," his mother Ba'u (the *Bôhu* of Genesis i. 2 ; i.e. " the Void," " Chaos " ; cf. the Indian Mother of the gods, Aditi, " the expanse," " the infinite ") was often styled " the sacred cow," and a cow was her symbol. Asari himself was also called " the Ram " (*alim*,[1] *ilim.*) All this may be compared with the animal-worship of Egypt, but doubtless these names were in large measure figurative. Asari or Marduk had many lofty titles, which serve to teach us what was believed about him. He is often called *Asari gal dug* [2] (" Asari who is good," or " the good person," though others render " the prince who does good to men "), and also " the life " (*tilla*). One of his special titles was *Bulluṭu*, " the Vivifier, the

[1] E.g., in *W.A.I.*, vol. ii., p. 55, col. 2, line 69. En Lil was also styled " the Ram."

[2] Ibid., lines 64–68.

Life-giver " (hence *Belteshazzar*, i.e., *Bulluṭu-šar-uṣur*, " May Merodach preserve the king "), and he is also called " lord of the bright charm, vivifier of the dead," the " merciful one, with whom it is to cause to live," " the god who by his might causeth the dead to live," besides other appellations such as " eldest son of the Abyss, mighty one of the gods, the great lord, prince of heaven and earth, king of heaven and earth, leader of the gods, establisher of the laws of the Abyss, lord of the ordinances of heaven and earth, king of the gods, lord of lords, begetter of wisdom, fixer of fates, warrior, strengthener of the gods, maker of the gods, begetter of the gods, renewer of the gods, the merciful lord who loves to cause the dead to live," and it is said of him that " what proceedeth out of his mouth is not overthrown." He is also called simply " God " (*Îlu*). The other deities seem gradually to have receded into the background in Babylon, leaving him as their representative. Of course the worshippers of certain other gods in Mesopotamia gave just as lofty titles to their own favourite deities. Thus Sin, the Moon-god, and Ba'u, the Goddess of the Void, are also said to " cause to live," and of Nabu (Nebo) too it is said that he could " give life to the dead." But this does not lessen the significance of the fact that all this should have been said of Asari or Merodach, who, in a celebrated Babylonian epic, is stated to have destroyed Ti'âmat (the monster which represented the deep), and made earth and sky out of her remains. With the assistance of Aruru, his consort, (or one of his consorts : Ishtar and Ṣarpanîtum—" the Shining," i.e. the Dawn—were also at times ascribed to him) he made mankind. Hence he held the " tablets of destiny " and became supreme. Zimmern is inclined to identify Marduk with Adapa, the first man ; but this is hardly consistent with the undoubted fact that he was the god of the rising sun, and probably of the setting sun too. Yet as Adapa was the first to die, and the sun dies every evening, there was some remote connexion possible to the imagination. We know how in India the first man, Yama, became ruler of the dead and also of the moon, though not of the sun. Asari or Merodach had a grand Temple (*E-šag-ili*, " the house of the high head ") in Babylon, and it was sometimes spoken of as his tomb. As therefore the Sun-god died and yet came to life every morning, being born afresh from the Heavenly Abyss, men felt that he might have more compassion on and sympathy with them as mortals and fated to die than the other gods could have. Hence they trusted that he would either restore them to health when sick or give them entrance to another life after death. In both senses he was said to be good to men and to " cause the dead to live." In Babylon we meet with no signs of belief in a resurrection of mankind, and we can hardly apply this term to the daily rising of the sun.

An attempt has been made to prove that the Babylonians thought of Merodach as having left them for a long time and as about finally to return, like Baldr, Lemenik and Arthur. But this does not agree with his being admittedly a Sun-god. The only passage quoted in support of the suggestion is one which, literally translated, runs thus : " Unto the futurity of men, in the growing old of days, let him rise : he shall not desist : let him rule unto eternity." [1] The evident meaning of

---

[1] K. 8,522, reverse, lines 10 and 11 (published in part xiii. of *Cuneiform Texts in British Museum*, plate 27) : *ah-ra-taš niši, la-ba-riš um-me, liš-ši-wa la uk-ta-li, li-bi-il ana ṣa-a-ti.*

this sentence in a paean in praise of Merodach, as Sun-god and Creator, is that it is hoped and believed that future generations of men, age after age, may see the Sun rise without ceasing day by day, dispensing light and life, as it is elsewhere said, " O Asari . . . eldest son of the Abyss, to give brightness to man and animal is thine," or, to adopt the Semitic rendering, " O Merodach, eldest son of the Abyss, thine it is to brighten and to cleanse." [1]

Merodach was in a sense, then, regarded by the Babylonians as a " Saviour," though not actually so called. He was their chief, though by no means their only, god : and his might and mercy were shown by his being men's creator and healer, and the bestower of future life.

There is some evidence in favour of the view that the Babylonians had in very early times a higher and more spiritual conception of Marduk-Asari than as a Sun-god. Professor Hommel says that it was " to make them more cognizable to the senses " that Ea was represented by the Moon-god, and Bel by the Wind-god ; and probably it was for the same reason that Marduk became a god of the sun, and even the planet Jupiter. Their being early called by animal names may be another attempt of the same kind, or it may be figurative. But in each case it shows that religion, in Babylonia as elsewhere, was subject to corruption and degradation.

Another great Deliverer is found in Egypt in the person of the god Osiris. He and his son Horus were among the chief deities of the " dynastic " Egyptians, the Semitic conquerors from Arabia and farther East who in very early times took possession of Egypt, subduing and ultimately being absorbed in the indigenous population.

---

[1] *W.A.I.*, vol. ii., p. 18, col. i., line 57.

It is now known that Osiris (called by the Egyptians
Àsàr or 'Iš-'ir) was really identical with the Šumerian
Asari (Merodach), of whom we have already spoken.
The name is precisely the same : the ideographs by
which the god was usually represented were in Egypt
a throne and an eye (𓁹), and the Šumerian god was
denoted by a combination of two cuneiform signs which
originally signified also an eye and a throne (⌐⊓,

"seat," and ⟨⌐ , "eye " ; in composition ⊏⟨⊢ ,
"Asari" : vide *W.A.I.*,[1] vol. ii., p. 18, l. 57, and
Hommel, *Sumerische Lesestücke*, p. 3, no. 31). Asari
in Babylonia was, as we have said, *Amar-dugga*, " the
good youth " ; and one of Osiris' appellations was *Un-
nefer*, " the Good Being." Professor Sayce also refers
to the fact that Osiris is often styled *Àti*, " the Prince,"
which is the very meaning of " Asari " in Šumerian.   But
there is a difference between Osiris in Egypt and Asari-
Marduk in Babylonia, in that Osiris was supposed to
be *dead* in body, and was hence called the " god of the
still heart," while Asari was always believed to be alive.
Osiris was " Chief of the Underworld " and ruler of the
dead, while Asari ruled the visible world of the living.
Yet both were distinctly Sun-gods, for Osiris was often
identified with Rā' and Seker.   Osiris gave life to the
dead in the sense of giving them conscious existence
in the Underworld, just as Merodach did.   It is noteworthy that, at least from the fifth dynasty to the very
latest times, the Egyptians always held Osiris to be king

---

[1] I.e. Rawlinson's *Western Asiatic Inscriptions.*

and god of the dead. More than this, " Egyptian writers always assume "—and even assert—" the identity of the blessed dead with their god " [1] Osiris.

Plutarch has told us the story of how Osiris had been murdered and mutilated by his brother Typhon (Set), and the Egyptian *Book of the Dead* assumes throughout the truth of this myth. His mummified body rested in the city of Ôn (Heliopolis).[2] As therefore it was preserved from decay, the deceased Egyptian is represented as desiring that his own body also may be preserved from corruption by Osiris (with whom, body and soul, he declares himself to be identified) and " may germinate," [3] thus producing the *sā'ḥu*, or " spiritual body " (as the word has been paraphrased—somewhat rashly perhaps). As " governor of Åmenti," the Underworld,[4] Osiris had power to cause men and women to be born again into the life beyond the grave. The Egyptians believed that the gods possessed bodies as material as those of men, and that equally required embalmment to preserve them from decay after death.

The expression " resurrection " is often employed rather carelessly in connexion with Osiris. But, as has been said, the Egyptian texts continually declare that Osiris' body is still dead and in its tomb,[5] and that the preservation of the mummies of his worshippers is dependent upon this fact, for they are said to be identified with his

---

[1] Budge, *Book of the Dead*, Introduction, p. lxxix.

[2] *Book of the Dead*, cap. clxii., *fin.* Others held that it was buried at Abydos, others somewhere else.

[3] Op. cit., cap. cliv.

[4] Åmenti, the realm of the dead, means either " the Western " or " the Hidden." Its supposed situation varied, and was not always thought to be below the ground.

[5] On Amélineau's supposed discovery of the place where

mummy.   "The educated Egyptian never believed that the material body would rise again," [1] but he did believe that, as King in the Underworld, Osiris gave new life in that region to his worshippers.   He alone of all the greater gods had been put to death.   Hence his devotees held that they might confidently count upon his sympathy with themselves in having to taste of death and to undergo all the perils to which their dark journeyings in the unseen world would expose them.

Dr. Budge's recent exhaustive study of *Osiris and the Egyptian Resurrection* casts much fresh light on the subject, even if we are unable to accept all his deductions. He argues that the worship of Osiris is very ancient— in fact pre-dynastic—in Egypt, whereas that of Rā' was apparently introduced in the time of the fifth dynasty. Dr. Budge holds that Osiris was at one time regarded as the Moon-god, and only much later associated with the Sun.   He denies the Asian origin of Osiris-worship and says it was purely African.   Osiris may have been an ancient King [2] of Abydos or some other place in Upper Egypt, deified after death.   His worship gradually

---

Osiris was buried, see his *Le Tombeau d'Osiris*, Paris, 1899 ; also Budge's *History of Egypt*, vol. i., pp. 11–20 ; and also an article in the *Times* of May 29, 1912.   Budge gives good reason to believe that the tomb which M. Amélineau explored was a *copy* of the tomb of an early Egyptian monarch called *Khent*, but that, as early as the sixth dynasty, the Egyptians themselves (misled by the fact that one of Osiris' titles was *Khent n Amenti*, "Ruler of the Underworld ") actually fancied that this was Osiris' tomb. The important point to notice is that it is hence evident that the Egyptians did not believe that Osiris had returned to life, but that his embalmed body still lay in this tomb at Abydos.

[1] Budge, *Introduction*, p. lxxxvi.

[2] This, however, seems hardly possible, if we consider what has been said above.

spread, taking the place of that of the other ancestral
spirits. Though long associated with the offering of
human sacrifices, the religion of Osiris very slowly succeeded in extinguishing the cannibalism at one time
prevalent. Dr. Budge continually speaks of the " resurrection " of Osiris, yet occasionally we are permitted to
see how inapplicable the word is to what was believed
to have happened to him. [1] " Osiris the god . . . had
lived in a body which had suffered and died, and had
been mutilated, and had, after reconstitution, been
raised from the dead by the god incarnate in it " (or
rather by his son Horus), " and had passed into heaven.
. . . Osiris was white, and was the personification of
good, Set was black (or red) and was the personification
of evil. These two gods fought each other continually,
and at length Set killed the mortal body of Osiris."
The latter rose " from the dead in a transfigured body,"
as we learn from texts as old as the sixth dynasty,
about 3500 B.C. " Somehow and somewhere the belief
arose that this particular god-man Osiris had risen from
the dead as the result of a series of magical ceremonies
which were performed by Horus, his son, under the
direction of the great magician Thoth, and with the
help of the embalmer or medicine-man Anubis." The
method in which, according to some texts, Horus restored
Osiris to life was by giving him his own eye, in which
Horus' life dwelt. Even as early as Pepi I's time, Osiris
was identified with the grain-god Neprà, at least very
probably. Dr. Budge gives pictures of Osiris' body
being put together and coming to life, and of the ladder

[1] *Osiris and the Egyptian Resurrection*, vol. i., pref., pp. xxi.-
xxv., and pp. 22, 80, 82, 83.

by which, with the assistance of certain other gods, he
was enabled to climb up into the sky, where at one time
the Egyptians supposed the abode of the happy deceased
to be, though at other times they imagined that it was
among the islands of Lake Victoria Nyanza.

A good deal of this whole theory of belief in Osiris'
"resurrection" is, quite logically, deduced from what
the Pyramid Texts say of Kings Pepi I and Tetà.   These,
like all true worshippers of Osiris, are stated to have
been identified with Osiris after their deaths, so that
what happened to Osiris in that existence happened to
these kings also.   Accordingly we read, "What Horus
hath done for Osiris, he hath done for this Pepi."[1]   But
Pepi's body was *not* supposed to have come to life and
risen from the dead, for we read, [2] "There is no proof
that they" (the Egyptians) "ever expected the physical
body to rise again ; on the contrary, the texts state
clearly that 'the soul is in heaven, *the body is in the
earth*' (Pepi I, line 85), and 'thy essence is in heaven,
thy body in the earth' (Pepi I, line 304). . . .   These
statements taken together prove that the Egyptians
believed that some kind of body rose from the dead and
continued its existence in the Other World."   Yet it is
clear that the Egyptians *did not believe* in the "resurrection" of Osiris in the sense in which we Christians believe
in the Resurrection of Christ.   They thought, apparently,
that Pepi's *sā'ḥu*, or "spiritual body," had entered
heaven, but they knew that his fleshly body lay embalmed
in his tomb.   As Horus had done for Pepi all that he
had done for Osiris, it followed that, just as did Pepi's,

---

[1] Pepi I's *Pyramid Texts*, line 191 ; quoted vol. ii., p. 309.
[2] Vol. ii., p. 123.

so Osiris' material body also still lay in its tomb, though *in another form* he had come to life. That this explanation is the right one is clear from the fact that at least very many of the Egyptian mummies had buried with them texts stating *their* identification with Osiris, though the mummy was not supposed to have come back to life on earth. Another fact which supports our contention is that [1] " the bull of Apis was believed to be an incarnation of Osiris, and to contain his soul. The appearance of a new Apis-bull was regarded as a new manifestation of Osiris upon earth." Once more, [2] " Osiris was the symbol of the African conception of resurrection and immortality, and from first to last his worship was characterized by customs and rites and ceremonies which were purely African." Among all the wealth of illustrations of Egyptian rites and beliefs, however, which Dr. Budge adduces from modern African religions, he nowhere produces any which show that the latter contain the doctrine that an ancient king rose from the dead in his material body. We must therefore carefully guard against being misled by the expression " the resurrection of Osiris."

It may be added that " there is nothing in the Texts which justifies the assumption that Osiris knew that he would rise from the dead and that he would become the king and judge of the dead, or that the Egyptians believed that Osiris died on their behalf and rose again in order that they also might rise from the dead." [3]

There was no belief that Osiris would ever return to this world. It is true that in a recent attempt at trans-

[1] Vol. i., p. 60. [2] Vol. i., p. 347.
[3] Vol. i., p. 312.

lating *The Burden of Isis*, the words *iu-f pu* at the end of certain chants (pp. 27 and 49) are incorrectly rendered, " Lo ! he comes ! " ; but this error is corrected in another place (p. 58), where the proper translation, " It is finished " (i.e. the book), is given instead.[1] The words mean " It has come," i.e. the conclusion of the book (cf. the Latin " explicit "). Hence Osiris differed from the much later (and post-Christian) Arthur and Baldr in this respect at least, that his worshippers hoped to go to him and become assimilated with (and perhaps absorbed into) him, but had no expectation of his coming back to them. It is well to call attention to this, because such errors in translation, and carelessness in the use of phrases elsewhere used in another connexion, are apt to mislead men into fancying resemblances, or even identity, where nothing of the kind really exists.

Turning to India, we there find more than one deity in whose assistance great reliance was (and still is) placed. Perhaps the most noteworthy of these is Kṛishṇa, " the black," whose worship was probably borrowed by the Âryans from the aborigines whom they conquered and subjected. A great deal has been written about Kṛishṇa in modern times. Some have entitled him an " Indian Christ," and have endeavoured to persuade their readers that much of the Gospel portraiture of our Lord is derived from India. Among others, the notorious Jacolliot, Dr. Marius, and Schuré, have drawn up accounts of Kṛishṇa, professedly from Indian sources, each of which accounts Prof. de Harlez is perfectly justified in saying, " All that in general is nothing but a tissue of lies. All

---

[1] See the end of, e.g., the *Papyrus Prisse*, and note in Budge, *History of Egypt*, vol. ii., pp. 79, 80.

at least is falsified in essence." Modern Hindû writers, such as Muralidhur Râya, Jñânendranâtha Mitra, and Bâlarâma Mallika, who have composed works in English in glorification of Krishna, have never ventured to imitate the European authors we have mentioned in their daring and unscrupulous mendacity. Other European writers on the same subject have exercised a perverted ingenuity in collecting what they, perhaps honestly, regard as evidence in favour of the influence which Krishnaism, in their opinion, has had on Christianity. As de Harlez says, " How sad it is to see men of intelligence and of good faith led astray by these unhealthy productions, which have nothing scientific about them but the appearance, and which know how to remove all distrust by the audacity of their affirmations ! "

The Sanskrit authorities [1] for the story of Krishna are the Harivamsa, the Agni Purâna, the Vishnu Purâna, the Bhâgavata Purâna, and the Mahâbhârata. An episode in the latter, the famous Bhagavad Gîtâ, teaches the eclectic philosophy of the system, which is as far

[1] Reference may also be made to the Taitarîya Âranyaka, the Âtharva Sañhitâ, and the eleventh chapter of the Lalita Vistara. In the much earlier Chhândogya Upanishad (iii., 17, 6) the following passage occurs : " Ghora, the descendant of Angiras, having declared this " (the preceding mystical lore) " to Krishna, the son of Devakî, said to him that " (which, when he heard) " he became free from thirst " (i.e., desire) ; " viz., ' Let a man at the time of his death have recourse to these three texts : Thou art the Undecaying, Thou art the Imperishable, Thou art the subtle Principle of Breath.' " If this Krishna is the same as the one mentioned in our other authorities, it is the earliest known reference to him : but the Krishna here mentioned seems to be a devotee, not a god. The Brâhmans do not identify the one with the other.

removed from the Christian as it is possible to imagine. Perhaps the only point in which they at all agree is the importance ascribed in the one to Faith, in the other to *Bhakti*, devotion. The Indian tale of Krishna is briefly as follows.

Vishnu plucked out two of his own hairs, one white and the other black, and said, " These my hairs shall go down to the Earth and relieve her of the burden of her distress. . . . This black hair of mine shall become incarnated in the eighth conception of the goddess-like Devakî, wife of Vasudeva, and shall destroy Kañsa, who is the demon Kâlanemi." Devakî, cousin of the tyrant Kañsa, had already borne to her husband Vasudeva six sons, who were in reality the offspring of the demon Hiranya-Kašipu, introduced into her womb by Yoga-nidrâ at Vishnu's command.   At the time of his marriage, Vasudeva had promised to hand over each of his children to Kañsa to be put to death, as soon as it should be born. This he had done, and all six had been slain ; for the tyrant feared Nârada's prophecy that one of Devakî's children would slay him.   Her seventh son was Bala-râma, who was white, and was the incarnation of Vishnu's white hair : the eighth son was Krishna.   At the time of his birth his parents were in confinement, to prevent the expected child from escaping death.   Krishna appeared as a four-armed figure in the sky in the middle of the night, and was born with four arms, but through *mâyâ* (illusion) appeared to have only two.   His father placed him for safety with Yašodâ, wife of the herdsman Nanda, who had just borne a girl, and gave the female infant to Devakî.   Kañsa, hearing this child's cries, seized it and dashed it against a stone, saying to Devakî, " The child of thy eighth conception is my death."   But the little girl flew up to the sky, telling the tyrant that the boy who would destroy him, and thus " rid the earth of her burden," was already born. Balarâma and Krishna grew up as cowherd boys at Gokula, exposed to many dangers, not least so when their foster father Nanda was absent at Mathurâ paying his taxes. But Krishna killed Pûtanâ, a female demon sent by the king to slay him. When sucking one day, Krishna " yawned, and revealed to his wondering mother the entire universe in his little mouth." [1] An evil spirit (*asura*) in the form of a heron swallowed him, but had to let him go. Krishna seized the bird by the beak and tore him in two. A python next swallowed Krishna, and his little playmates, but Krishna killed him, and then by a glance of his eye he restored to life his comrades whom he found to be dead. He overcame the huge serpent Kalya that dwelt in Lake Yamunâ, near Vrindâvana, and forced him to take refuge in the sea. Indra was angry with Krishna, and sent a great rain-storm to test his divinity ; but Krishna held up Mount Govardhana on one finger for seven days over the cowherds, and thus preserved them from it. He slew a washerman who refused to surrender to him some clothes which he desired to possess, and then cured a deformed girl. The latter tale is thus related in the Vishnu Purâna :—

" Krishna saw a young girl who was crooked, carrying a pot of unguent. Krishna addressed her in sweet words and said, ' For whom are you carrying that unguent ? Tell me, lovely maiden, tell me truly.' Being thus kindly addressed by him, and being attracted by his kindness and well disposed towards Hari,[2] the hump-

[1] Vide p. 89.
[2] Another name for Vishnu, who is identified with Krishna.

backed girl also replied pleasantly to him, ' Do you not
know, my lord, that my name is Tribakrâ ? I am the
servant of Kañsa and am appointed to prepare his per-
fumes.' " At Krishna's request she gave Krishna and
Balarâma some of the unguent. " Then Krishna, skilled
in the art of healing, took hold of her under the chin
with the thumb and two fingers and lifted up her head,
while with his feet he pressed down her feet, and in this
way he made her straight. Being thus rendered straight
she became the most beautiful of damsels." The rest
of the tale introduces the licentious element that pervades Krishna's whole story : we therefore omit it, as
we do his amours with the cowherds' daughters.

Afterwards Krishna fought and slew the mad elephant
Kuvalayapîda, and then in Kañsa's presence he and
Balarâma encountered in a wrestling match and slew
the wrestlers Chânûra, Mushtika, and others. Krishna
then put Kañsa to death and made his own father Vasudeva King of the Yâdavas instead, his capital being
Mathurâ (the present Mattra). Krishna defeated the
demon Naraka. He married more than 16,000 damsels,
of whom Rukminî and seven others were his favourites,
and begat 180,000 sons, who all perished in battle with
one another or at their father's hands. Mounted on the
wonderful bird Garuda and accompanied by Satyabhâmâ,
one of his wives, Krishna met and defeated the Air-god
Indra in battle in the latter's own realm, bringing back
as spoils the " Mountain of Gems " and the famous
Pârijâta tree. On another occasion he went on Garuda
to " the city of the celestials " to restore to the goddess
Aditi the earrings she had given him. He learnt the
art of war from the Rishi Sâmdîpani, and he promised
to reward the latter by restoring to life his son who had

M

been drowned. The story goes that Krishna demanded the boy's restoration from Varuna, god of the ocean, but was told that he was not in his keeping, but in that of the demon Panchajana. After a fierce struggle he defeated and slew this Daitya Pañchajana, and then proceeded to seek the boy in Yama's abode, Yamapura, in the Underworld. The dread king of the dead prostrated himself and yielded up the 'captive. Another visit from Krishna resulted in the surrender to him of his six brothers whom Kañsa had slain. When the wife of his nephew, Abhimanyu, gave birth to a dead child, Krishna gave it life. In the Bhagavad Gîtâ he acts as Arjuna's charioteer, and urges him to fight and slay in battle those of his kindred who were opposed to him, arguing that, because of the transmigration of souls, they could not really be slain.

The death of Krishna occurred in the following way. "Krishna sat engaged in meditation, placing his foot upon his knee. Then there came a hunter named Jâra." . . . Mistaking Krishna's foot for part of a deer, he shot his arrow into the sole of it. "Approaching his mark, he saw the four-armed King, and, falling at his feet, repeatedly besought his pardon, exclaiming, ' I have done this deed unknowingly, thinking I was aiming at a deer. Have pity on me who am consumed by my crime, for thou art able to consume me.' " Krishna pardoned him and sent him to " the region of the celestials " on a celestial car. Krishna died of his wound. Arjuna erected a funeral pyre for him, and on it Rukminî, Revatî, and six others of his wives were burned alive with the corpse. Vasudeva and Devakî thereupon " entered the fire " also.

We have thought it best to relate this tale at some

length, because so many garbled accounts of it are
prevalent in Europe. Some have endeavoured to prove
that it is very ancient ; but there is no trace of it in the
Vedas, though Krishna himself may have been worshipped by the aborigines long before the Âryans admitted
him to their Pantheon. The story which we have given
is found only in the Purânas and the Epics, which are
of uncertain date, possibly in some parts going back to
the sixth century of our era. Attempts have been made
to show that the grammarian Patañjani knew something
of Krishna's killing Kañsa ; but as this author wrote
his *Mahâbhâshya* (a commentary on Pânini's grammatical
Sûtras and on Kâtyâyana's *Vârttikas*) a considerable
time after the composition of Pânini's work, and as
Pânini is held by Weber and others to have lived at earliest
about the end of the first Christian century, that circum-
stance is not of much consequence, nor does it prove
the existence of the rest of the tale at such a date. The
fact that Varuna is represented as a god of the sea like
Poseidon, and Yama as ruling a region of the lower world,
is conclusive proof of a comparatively late date for at
least those parts of the tale that relate to Krishna's
dealings with these beings : for in the *Rig-Veda* Varuna
is the supreme Âryan deity, the god of the sky, becoming
an evil deity of the sea only much later.[1] Similarly in
Vedic times Yama's realm was in the sky,[2] not in the
gloomy regions of the Underworld. De Gubernatis has

---

[1] The *one* passage in which in the *Rig-Veda* Varuna is styled
Sindhu-pati (" lord of the river or ocean ") is *Rig-Veda*, vii.,
64, 2. The contrast to later usage in this respect is striking and
significant. It is noteworthy that Ea, like Varuna, was first lord
of the heavenly ocean, and afterwards of the sea.

[2] Cf. *Rig-Veda*, vii., 55, 2–4 ; x., 14 ; x., 154, etc.

seen in some of the tales about Krishna contributions
from " the knowledge of Christ which had reached India,
and which appears to me " (he says), " as to Weber, to
have supplied Krishna with a part of his teaching and
different episodes of his life." De Harlez, Hopkins, and
many other scholars agree with this view. The latter
says of these supposed " coincidences," " Whatever is
most marvellous in the accounts of Christianity finds
itself here reproduced in Krishnaism," and again : " The
outer Christianity reflected in the Purânic legends of
Krishna is as palpable as it is shocking. Shocking, for
not only are miracles treated grotesquely, but everything
that is meant spiritually in the Occident is interpreted
physically and carnally." [1]   No one who honestly
examines the Sanskrit authorities on the subject can
possibly fancy that a single Gospel narrative could conceivably have been derived from any of these fantastic
stories about Krishna, though he may perhaps doubt
whether any of the latter are due to distorted reports
of the former. It is perhaps hard to learn any lesson
in Comparative Religion from Krishna, except how terribly
corrupt certain forms of religion may readily become.
The prevalence of Krishna-worship in India to-day,
however, tends at least to show how badly men need a
Helper and a Saviour, when they can devote themselves,
" body, mind and property," to Krishna and to his later
supposed incarnations, often the vilest and most licentious
of men.

It is a relief to turn from such a Deliverer—if in any
sense Krishna can be termed such—to another great
Indian character—this time an historical personage,

---

[1] Hopkins, *Religions of India*, pp. 430, 431.

Gautama Buddha, who was born in Nipâl about 557
B.C. and died about 477 B.C.   In later times and in the
books of the Northern Buddhists wonderful tales were
told about the Buddha, but it seems (as we have seen)
that his birth occurred when his mother Mâyâ was about
forty-five years of age, after some thirty-three years of
married life.   She died seven days later.   The perverse
ingenuity of modern days has endeavoured to turn this
into a Virgin-birth, and has succeeded as well as in other
attempts to deduce the historical facts of the Gospels
from the latest fables which after-ages told about Buddha.
His teaching differed as much from that of Christ as did
his history.   On this we need not dwell.   Suffice it to
say that genuine Buddhism is in most respects the very
antithesis of Christianity.[1]

Buddha's father, Šuddhodana, was a wealthy land-
owner.   His son's name was Siddhârtha, to which the
family name, Gautama, was added.   The title Buddha
(" the Knower ") was given when he took upon himself
the office of Teacher.   Siddhârtha married at least one
wife (Buddhist accounts say 40,000, or 80,000), and his
only recorded son was Râhula, born when his father was
twenty-nine years of age.   Siddhârtha then left home,
wife and son, to become an anchoret, hoping thus to
obtain peace of mind.   After persisting in this course
for seven years, he at last discovered its futility.   Soon
afterwards while sitting under a *pîpal* tree near Uruvelâ,
engaged in meditation, he suddenly imagined that he
had attained to omniscience, and had discovered the
reason of human suffering and the way to end it.   This
he summed up in the " Four Noble Truths," which teach

---

[1] See my *Noble Eight-fold Path* (C.M.S. House).

that all existence is, and must ever be, painful; that attachment to existence causes this suffering to continue; that by destroying this attachment (" thirst ") existence can be made to cease; and that only by following the Noble Eight-fold Path laid down by the Buddha can any existent being attain Nirvâṇa, the state of " extinction " of the passions, and ultimately of existence itself. This is not religion but philosophy. Buddha did not acknowledge that there was a Creator of the universe, and he taught that the popular deities of the vulgar needed his method of deliverance as much as did men. His life was spent in teaching this dreary philosophy, and he died through some error of diet at the age of eighty years. His body was cremated, and he ceased to exist, according to the belief of his earliest followers. Many legends have naturally sprung up about him, and his system has grown into a number of different religions, for the Buddhism of Tibet differs much from that of Ceylon, and that again from the Buddhism of Japan. But it is only by the unrestrained exercise of the imagination that the few incidents that are known of his life can be compared with those in the life of our Lord. Comparative Religion can learn little from original Buddhism, except that man needs a Saviour, and that Buddha failed to satisfy that need.

If we now turn to Persia, we there find another of the greatest of human teachers, Zoroaster, or, as he is called in the Avesta, Zarathuštra (owner of the " yellow camel "). From what is said in the Artâ-Vîrâf Nâmak, it seems that his religion arose about the middle of the seventh century before Christ. The Avesta traces his descent back for ten generations to his forefather, Spitama. Zoroaster's father was Pôurushaspa, and his mother Dughdhôva.

Nothing marvellous is related of his birth. He was the third of five brothers, and was born to reward his father for his piety in offering oblations of haoma-juice. Zoroaster's wife, Hvôvî, was daughter of Frashaostra, the brother of Jâmâsp, minister of Vîshtâspa (Hystaspes, Gushtâsp), King of Bactria. The Avesta gives the names of the three sons and the three daughters born to Zoroaster, as well as the prophecy of those to be born in ages then future. His birthplace was probably Ragha (now Rai or Shâh 'Abdu'l 'Azîm, some five and a half miles south of Tehrân). According to tradition, he was driven from home when a young man and took refuge at the court of Vîshtâspa, who, with his queen Hutaosa, became his patron. Frashaostra was one of his earliest disciples, and helped to spread the new faith, which is said to have been revealed to Zoroaster by Ahura-Mazdâ on Mt. Ushi-darena in Sîstân. The *Gâthâs*, or Hymns, the oldest part of the Avesta, are probably of Zoroaster's own composition. They show that, besides Ahura-Mazdâ, he worshipped the Amesha Speñtas and other good Powers, and attributed much efficacy to charms (*mâthras*). The Avesta tells us of the questions he asked Ahura-Mazdâ and the answers he received. Tradition says he was killed by a Turanian at the age of seventy-eight.

In process of time many fables were told about him. Most of these are given in the Zarâtusht Nâmah, composed in A.D. 1278 from older works. He laughed when born, whereas all other children cry, and his smile lightened the house. A king, skilled in magic, Dûrâsarûn by name, tried to cut the infant in two with his sword, but his arm withered. Magicians endeavoured to kill the child by throwing him into a great fire, by exposing him to be trodden underfoot by cattle and horses, and to be

torn in pieces by wolves, but he escaped from every danger. He had seven conferences with Ormazd (Ahura-
Mazdâ) in ten years, visiting heaven under Bahman's
guidance. Returning with the Avesta he went to Bactria and taught his Law to Vîshtâspa. Some few of
these stories existed in Pliny's time, but none of them
occur even in the latest parts of the Avesta itself. Their
comparatively late date being thus evident, they need
not any longer detain us.

The Zoroastrian faith in its purity was a reformation,
an endeavour to recall the nation to the higher religion
of earlier days and to get men to reject the corruptions
which had gradually crept into it. Except in thus teaching what certainly contained not a few elements of truth,
Zoroaster was not a " Saviour," and made no claim to
be anything but a man with a Divine commission, to teach
the truth and banish the " lie." Îrân has never produced a greater man.

The corrupt heathenism which for a time Zoroastrianism in some measure displaced acknowledged many
deified powers of Nature as gods. One of the mightiest
of these gods was Mithra, the Sun-god, or the spirit ruling
the solar orb. Zoraastrianism, as taught in the Avesta,
admitted Mithra's greatness and honoured him much,
but must have lowered his rank, for it did not admit him
into the number of the Amesha-speñtas, though these in
the Avesta represent the Âdityas in the *Rig-Veda*, one
of whom was Mitra, as Mithra is there named. Mithra,
in the Avesta, is sometimes said to have been created by
Ahura-Mazdâ of equal dignity with himself.[1] This,
however, was not peculiar to him, for much the same
thing is said of Tishtrya [2] (Sirius, the Dog-star) also. It

---

[1] E.g., Yasht x., 1.　　[2] Yasht viii., 50 *sqq.*

probably means that the rivalry between these deities in
the minds of their respective worshippers could be kept
from breaking out only by placing them on an equality
with one another. Mithra punished untruth and breach
of faith, rode over the world in his chariot with one wheel
(the sun), aided Ahura-Mazdâ in his contest with Añrô-
Mainyuš (Ahriman), and was *one* of the three judges of
the dead (Sraosha and Rashnu being the other two)
before whom men's spirits appeared ere crossing the
Chinvaṭ-bridge. Artaxerxes Mnemon and Artaxerxes
Ochus in their inscriptions pray to him, as well as to
Ahura-Mazdâ and Anâhita, for the preservation of the
realm. As Sun-god, Mithra presided over fertility in
men and animals, as did the goddess Anâhita, originally
the guardian and representative of a sacred stream.
Their association together shows that Mithraism very
soon became morally corrupt, as indeed we know from
history it did.

Mithra-worship spread far beyond the limits of Persia,
at first throughout Asia Minor, Armenia, and Syria, and
then throughout a great part of the Roman Empire. It
was essentially in Imperial times a religion of soldiers,
and the legions carried it with them, through Gaul and
Germany, as far as Caledonia. It was closely connected
with the worship of Cybele and a great many other deities,
many of which were adored with shockingly immoral
rites. Human sacrifices seem sometimes to have been
offered to Mithra. Inscriptions in his underground
chapels style him " the unconquered Sun " and " the
Sun-god Mithra," and identify him with Hêlios.

We have no extant scriptures belonging to Western
Mithraism, but there seems reason to believe (from the
statements of various Greek and Latin writers) that

Mithra was said to have sprung from a rock. Sculptures represent him as thus coming forth as a youth in a Phrygian cap. As we have already pointed out, in Avestic Persian the word *asman* means " sky " as well as " rock," the firmament being conceived of as a solid mineral mass. Hence Mithra's birth from a rock denoted the daily birth of the Sun-god from the sky. Mithra is also represented as stabbing a bull, which probably signifies the earth, which is fertilized by the sun's darts or rays. He was regarded as a " middleman " between Ormazd and Ahriman, the Good and the Evil Principles. Mithraism had many strange, often cruel, rites. It seems to have taught transmigration and the immortality of the spirit. Modern theories as to its doctrines are largely founded upon imagination. Mithra, as a Sun-god, may be compared with Merodach and Osiris. It was not his part to save men from sin, but to punish liars and perjurers. In spite of many assertions to the contrary, Mithra was not supposed to have ever been a man, or to have been born of a Virgin, or to have died, been buried, or risen again; nor was his religion one " of inward holiness, of austere self-discipline and purity." |Nor, again, was he spoken of as the " Divine Word or Reason," or " the Incarnate Word." The attempt to represent Mithraism as strikingly similar to Christianity fails utterly when enquired into.[1] But, even if it had succeeded, we should still have had to remember that " Similarity of pattern between two plates, the one empty, the other full, does not fill the empty plate " (Moule : *The Splendour of a Great Hope,*

[1] Vide my paper on " Mithraism " in the forty-third volume of the *Journal of the Victoria Institute,* and also my *Mythic Christs and the True,* ch. i.

p. 20). The attempt to compare Mithra with Christ reminds us of an advertisement of a certain electric lamp, in which a picture of the earth shows one side brightly illuminated by that lamp and the other faintly lighted by the sun, the legend underneath being " his only rival."

Attis and Tammuz are two other forms in which the Sun-god was worshipped in Western Asia. Tammuz was also styled Adonis by the Greeks, through a misunderstanding of the title *Adônî* (" my lord ") by which he was addressed. Tammuz—in Sumerian *Dumu-zi-(Apzu)*, " Son of the Spirit (of the Abyss)," that is of the god Ea—was originally the sun at dawn, and therefore another form of Asari or Merodach. The probability is that in early times Tammuz and Asari were but two names of the same deity, the rising sun, and that the different legends that arose about them and made them in some measure separate deities were to a great degree due to local differences in the places in which their worship arose. Thus in the Âryan world Jupiter, Zeus, and Dyaus, are one and the same deity, though somewhat different tales are current about each of them. It was a true feeling, therefore, which, later, led people at Byblos and elsewhere in Phoenicia to identify Osiris (Asari) with Tammuz (Adonis).

Tammuz, from being the young Sun, came (as did Osiris in Egypt) to represent the fresh vegetation of the spring, brought up from the bosom of the earth by his fertilizing rays. Hence the fierce heat of summer, which dries up and withers vegetation, was the foe which every year slew him, according to the Babylonian myth. An early and popular belief in Babylonia was that Ishtar (Ashtoreth) went down to the abode of the dead, ruled over by Queen Allatu, to seek the *water* which alone could restore her dead lover, Tammuz, to life. Farther west, in Syria and the neighbouring regions, Tammuz or Adonis represented rather the vegetation of summer, which was killed by the " white tusk of the boar " of winter, i.e. the hoar frost. His lover, the goddess Aphroditê (Ishtar) bitterly lamented him, and made a flower spring from his blood. Another tale is that, when he was a child, Aphroditê entrusted him to Persephonê (Proserpine), goddess of the Lower World, to be brought up. When he grew up, Persephonê refused to let him return to Aphroditê on earth. An appeal to Zeus resulted in the decree that Adonis should spend a third of each year with each of the two rival goddesses, and what was left of it as he pleased. He decided to pass it in Aphroditê's company. Here again it is evident that we are dealing with a Nature-myth, as was fully recognized by the god's worshippers. It is well known that the conception of Adonis as the generative power in Nature, and especially in the sun, which causes vegetation to spring up, and that of Aphroditê as the receptive and parturient principle, led to the vilest rites and the most abominable immorality. But this is a general truth with regard to all systems in which the productive powers of Nature are adored.

Attis was a Phrygian deity whose name probably meant " Father." The myth represented him as born of a monster called Agdistis and a princess named Nana (" Mother "). Agdistis himself was born of a huge rock, thus reminding us of Mithra, his father being Zeus. As he thus sprang from the earth; fertilized by rain, he too, in all probability, represented the god of fertility. Attis is often held to be but another form of Agdistis. The fable of his association with the Earth-Mother, the

" Great Mother," Cybele, his self-mutilation and death, is well known and not very charming. Arnobius tells us that Zeus refused to restore Attis to life, but granted that his body should not decay, his hair should continue to grow, and his little finger should always keep on moving. Here we are reminded of the tale, told both in China and ancient Scandinavia, of the giant whose flesh became the soil and his hairs the plants which sprang up from it.

There can be no question that the worshippers of Tammuz and Attis adored what they knew to be the procreative element in Nature, personified in these gods. The phallic and other rites associated with their festivals clearly show this. It is equally evident that in neither case were these deities ever believed to have been men who had died.   Yet the very fact that by their " deaths " —though these were only figurative—these gods appealed in a special manner to men, conscious themselves of mortality, is a proof of men's need of some Divine Being, man as well as God, Who, having Himself suffered death and yet returned to life, could feel for them and save them. Of the existence of such a Being they had no knowledge, and yet instinct, or some higher impulse, led many a man in ancient days, and in lands far distant from one another, if not to hope for such a Deliverer, at least, feeling dimly conscious of his need, to

> Stretch lame hands of faith, and grope,
> And gather dust and chaff.

Yet the hope was in itself a prophecy, destined to fulfilment " in the fulness of time," and in this sense a vital part of the Divine education of the human race.

CHAPTER XII

Sin and its Remedy

ALL religions admit the existence of sin, though differing much as to its nature and remedy. The fact that such words as *bad, wicked, guilty*, occur in every language shows that conscience everywhere convicts man of sinfulness. That guilt in some considerable degree weighs on men's minds in all parts of the world is also clear from the universality of the institution of sacrifice, one of the most important of the objects of which is propitiation for sin. Universal experience teaches that there is need of some atonement for sin, otherwise peace of heart cannot be obtained. That sin is a reality is also shown to have been widely realized through the fact that every tribe or community has something of the nature of a code of ethics, more or less perfect, stating what deeds must not be done, and often prescribing the penalty for the transgression of the law. The earliest known code of laws is that of Ḥammurabi (Amraphel), but many or all of the individual enactments in that code go back to very remote times, and they were not codified until hoary antiquity had invested them with a recognized sacredness. The negative Confession in the *Book of the Dead* is doubtless very ancient, and it affords proof of what deeds the Egyptians of the early ages deemed particularly abominable in the eyes of the Judge of the Dead, Osiris.

The moral codes of various religions and different nations often agree with one another regarding certain actions which they condemn, yet strangely enough very evil deeds are sometimes permitted in certain cases, and even commended. Among the Dayaks of Borneo, for example, as among the Nâgas of Assam, and the Sioux of North America, a youth was not accounted a man and a warrior, or permitted to wed, until he had killed a human being, though to murder any member of one's own tribe was condemned and punished. The moral code of Buddhism in some respects resembles the last six prohibitions of the Mosaic " Ten Commandments," but it couples the use of " garlands, scents, unguents, ornaments and finery as adornments," the act of sleeping in " a high bed, a big bed," and that of accepting presents of gold and silver for one's own use, with theft, lying and unchastity as equally unbecoming. Yet transgression of these rules, and even of the " Four Prohibitions," [1] is not held to be a moral offence, though it is bad because it entails evil consequences on the transgressor and retards his attainment of Nirvâṇa. Buddhism has this in common with almost all other systems but the Christian, that it accounts certain perfectly innocent actions criminal, while it permits some wicked deeds with hardly a remonstrance. Thus for a *Bhikkhu* (" mendicant " or member of the Order of Monks) to return to family life is far more sinful than to be guilty of bestiality,[2] and to kill any animal, even a noxious insect, is a crime. A modern Hindû regards a

---

[1] See my *Noble Eight-fold Path* (C.M.S. House), p. 129.
[2] *Mahâvaggo* i., cap. 78, § 2.

breach of the rules of his caste as far more wicked than any moral offence. The *Hitopadeśa* teaches us how perverted men's minds are apt to become through false religious teaching, when it says, " The world follows a precedent, and does not take as an authority in religion a right-teaching bawd as it does a cow-killing Brâhman." [1] This shows that, in the mind of the writer, it was a far worse thing to kill a cow than to live by inciting to impurity.

Religions by no means agree in defining what sin is. Avoiding all technical language, it may be said that the ancient Greeks, and most Semites, thought that sin consisted in " missing the mark "—in failure to do what was expected of one. It was negatively bad, rather than positively so. The Egyptian, on the other hand, judging from the *Book of the Dead*, took, in theory at least, a much more serious view of sin. He " had no conception of repentance. At the Judgment which took place in the Hall of Osiris, he based his claim for admission into the kingdom of that god upon the fact that he had not committed certain sins." [2] However, he thought that his meritorious works would stand him in good stead, and he boasts of them before Osiris. " When he had any doubt about their power to deliver him finally from the hosts of darkness, he protected himself by means of amulets." In the *Book of Breathings* we find a man claiming to come before the gods of Ṭuat, or the Underworld, on the plea of his absolute sinlessness : [3] " There is neither any evil whatsoever nor any sin whatsoever with

[1] *Hitopadeśa*, Bk. i., fable 2.
[2] Budge, *Book of the Dead*, Translation, p. clxxi.
[3] Op. cit., p. cci.

him, and no accuser can stand [before him]." This does not show any very keen moral sense.

Hindûism and Buddhism in ancient times, though holding inaccurate notions of what actions were wrong and what right, yet admitted the serious consequences that must inevitably result from evil deeds, and sometimes from evil words and thoughts. This is clear from the doctrine of *Karma* (" deed "), in accordance with which every act, good or bad, had a certain " fruit," which the doer must " eat." Buddha taught that no repentance and no good deeds could undo or atone for evil conduct : it must work itself out here and hereafter to the bitter end. Yet genuine Buddhism denies that there is any distinction in *kind* between good and evil, admitting it only in *degree*. Thus black is but a delicate shade of white, vice a slightly modified form of virtue. This results from the absence of all belief in a God Who created the world, and to Whom His creatures are responsible for their obedience or disobedience to His laws.

The Muḥammadan view of sin is the very converse of this. According to Islâm, sin is the transgression of some quite arbitrary command of God. What is now a sin may not always have been one, and perhaps may become quite an innocent act in the future. It all depends upon a definite order issued by the irresponsible Despot Who rules the Universe, Who is accountable to no one and can do just as He pleases. Thus a Muslim holds that in New Testament times it was wrong to draw the sword for the spread of the faith, and it was still wrong in the early days of Islâm, while the precept " Let there be no compulsion in the religion " [1] was yet in force. But at a certain definite moment this was abrogated.

[1] Sûrah ii., 257.

Muḥammad became the " Prophet with the Sword," and thenceforth, in the opinion of Muḥammadans, it was the duty of earnest Muslims to spread their religion by war : " Fight ye against those who believe not in God nor in the Last Day, and who forbid not what God and His Apostle have forbidden, and who profess not the True Religion, from among those who have been brought the Book "—i.e. the Bible—" until they give the *jizyah*-tax out of hand and be brought low." [1]   So, again, it is now wrong for a Muslim to drink wine, but in the next world it will be right ; in fact, one of the joys of Paradise will be unlimited indulgence in drinking from rivers of wine, though no headaches will result therefrom.   There is the less excuse for such a defective conception of sin in Islâm, because it might have learnt something much loftier from the Judaism and Christianity with which, at its beginning, it came in contact, and from which it borrowed matters of little importance.

Yet, though the ancient non-Christian religions (to return to them) never attained any clear view of the real nature of sin, nevertheless conscience asserted itself most terribly in the minds of not a few of the men who professed those faiths.   An instance of this is afforded by the Greek conception of the *Nemesis* which punished arrogance and impiety towards the gods, and in that of the *Erinyes* (Furies) and the *Kêres*, avenging deities who pursued those guilty of matricide, parricide, perjury and other gross offences.   To avoid these justly angry goddesses was almost hopeless, though perchance escape from them might possibly be found within the precincts of Apollo's shrine at Delphi.   Classical authors sometimes tell us of the awfulness of remorse for crimes com-

[1] Sûrah ix., 29.

mitted and incapable of being atoned for. Juvenal's well-known picture of the unavailing agony which an offender might thus suffer is unsurpassed in ancient writers. That there was such a thing as moral evil could not therefore be denied, nor could it be doubted that sometimes, as in Nero's case, the terrible consciousness of one's crimes would haunt the perpetrator. Yet no realization of the true nature of sin seems to have been reached. What made the tortures of conscience, when awakened, the more frightful, was that neither reason nor religion could discover any satisfactory way of atoning for sin and of obtaining inward peace.

Even the greatest philosophers of the past failed to realize the true heinousness of sin, though at times they seem to have caught a glimpse of this, as by a flash of lightning. In such instances they start back, awed and astounded at the ghastly sight, but they fail to find a way of escape. At times they despairingly assert that no escape, no remedy, can possibly be found : that there is *no* power which can undo the past, which can cleanse the guilty conscience, or even enable the fallen to over- come vice and return to the path of virtue. At other times they either deny the existence of sin, or explain that evil has only a negative existence, or that good and evil are merely relative, and that no one does evil deeds purposely. Socrates thought that ignorance was the cause of wrong doing, and that, therefore, its cure was knowledge. The same idea tends to reassert itself to-day among those who do not accept Christian teaching, though they no longer hold, as he did, that a person who does wrong knowingly is a better man than one who does it in ignorance. Readers of Xenophon and Plato must notice how unconscious of the moral enormity of sexual vice Socrates showed himself to be. Yet Socrates, dim as his religious ideas were, had at least learnt that one should obey God rather than men. He may possibly owe this to Pythagoras, who taught that men are God's property and therefore should in all things obey Him. But what this meant, and how to do it, or how to obtain pardon for not doing what one should, neither philosopher could tell. Plato and Greek philosophers in general write many noble things about the beauty of virtue, but they nowhere show any true consciousness of what sin is. Plato often seems to regard it as a transgression of some rule of the state or body politic. His recommendation of the community of wives in his ideal Republic is of itself sufficient to prove a great degree of moral obliquity of vision. He agrees with Socrates as to the importance of knowledge, and thus reminds us of Buddha's condemnation of ignorance, though both philosophers used such terms with a purely technical meaning. Aristotle in this contradicts Plato, and holds that men become virtuous only through the practice of virtue. He admits that the intellect cannot itself impel men to right acts, and that by itself, though it observes and criticizes our conduct, it is impotent to produce anything practical. The motive-power of good conduct he finds in the affections.[1] The defect which very largely vitiates his system of ethics is his failure to recognize the existence of sin as such. Certain virtues he condemns as vices, as for instance, when he says that it is worthy of a slave not duly to revenge oneself for an injury.[2] The Stoics had far loftier ethical ideas. They regarded vice as the only evil, and spoke of the truly wise man as master of himself. Seneca saw

[1] *Eth. Nicom.*, vi., ii., 5.   [2] *Eth. Nicom.*, iv., v., 5–13.

that the recognition of sin is the beginning of salvation,[1]
and he occasionally uses language which recalls that of
St. Paul. Yet his idea of sin is very largely that it is
error through ignorance ; though how the man who knew
Nero, who had taught his imperial pupil and murderer
what he held to be right, and who himself wrote for Nero
his letter to the Senate in defence of the murder of Agrip-
pina, can really have thought so passes comprehension.
The Pantheism which underlay the whole Stoic philosophy effectually prevented men from realizing the true
nature of sin : for the history of morals clearly shows
that the due realization of the heinousness of sin is possible
only when men attain to a worthy conception of God and
a proper idea as to man's relation to Him.   This, in all
history, has never been at all adequately gained, except in
and through the Lord Jesus Christ. If, as we have been
told, the " man in the street to-day is not worrying about
his sins," the reason is that " God is not in all his thoughts."

If we turn from the Greek and Roman world to ancient
China, we see the same picture of moral obtuseness on
the one hand, of despair on the other. Confucius was
certainly not a religious man : he never appeals to the
duty of pleasing God, in fact he hardly ever mentions
Him, though he knew that He had been worshipped in
ancient times. Confucius never represents his ideal of
excellence, his " Superior man," as thinking of the duty
of doing the will of " Heaven."   Hence this philosopher
regarded sin as merely an offence against the State. Yet
he says, " Man is born for uprightness. If a man lose
his uprightness and yet live, his escape from death is a
mere accident." [2] He tells us that the steadfastly good

---

[1] Ep. 28.   [2] *Analects*, vi., 7.

man would rather encounter death itself than leave deeds of benevolence undone : yet he states that he had never met with a perfect man, with one who loved virtue as well as he did sensual pleasure. [1] " He adds the despairing opinion that the man who sins against Heaven has no place wherein to pray,[2] no posture, no position, no aspect, by which he can draw near and crave the pardon of offended Heaven." He has no suggestion for saving sinners or for raising the fallen.

Mencius held that man was inclined to what is good by his very nature, just in the same way that it is natural for water to flow downhill and not uphill. Of himself he says, " I love life, and I love righteousness : but, if I cannot retain the two, I will let life go and hold fast to righteousness." He held that benevolence would overcome malevolence, as water overcomes fire.[3] He admitted, however, that no teacher could supply his pupils with moral power so as to enable them to do what they had learnt to be right. Nor does he seem to have realized that outward rites fail to cleanse the heart, for he says, " Though a man be wicked, if he duly prepares himself by fasting and abstinence and purification by water, he may sacrifice to God (Shang-ti)." [4]

A later philosopher, Chwan-tsze, who commented on Laou-tsze's Taouism, recognizes sin as a transgression of the *Taou* or " Way," the course of Nature. [5] " But for this sin of the past, the barrier to reconciliation and reunion with Heaven, there is no promise in Taouism

---

[1] Moule, *The Splendour of a Great Hope*, p. 19.
[2] *Analects*, iii., 13.   [3] Moule, op. cit., p. 118.
[4] Giles, *Religions of Ancient China*, pp. 42, 43.
[5] Moule, op. cit., p. 86.

of repentance, atonement and pardon ; and without this the creed is hopeless and powerless, pathetic though its flutterings Godward are."

If we turn to Hegel, one of Germany's greatest philosophers, we do not find in him very much more help than in the philosophers of old. " Defects, error, sin, are for Hegel only imperfectly real. . . . All sin is for Hegel relatively good. . . . There is no trace in Hegel of any feeling of absolute humility and contrition of man before God. . . . Sin is a mere appearance. Like all appearances it is based on reality. But the reality it is based on is not sin. Like all reality, it is perfectly good. The sinfulness is part of the appearance." [1]

In this matter of sin and its remedy the Gospel succeeds where everything else has failed. The Christian view of sin is at once infinitely sterner and infinitely tenderer and more hopeful than any other : its remedy has succeeded in untold thousands, nay millions of cases, where everything else had failed. Sin is diagnosed as the condition of alienation [2] from God into which human nature has fallen, being perverted from its original harmony with the Divine Nature through its misuse of the Divine gift of freedom of will. As a perversion of man's true nature, Sin is necessarily injurious to man and hateful to God, Who is Holy, and Who loves His human creature, and hence desires to save him from guilt and ruin and restore him to peace and happiness. Certain thinkers [3] of old spoke of sins of thought and

---

[1] McTaggart, quoted by Orr, *Sin as a Problem of To-day*, pp. 79, 80.

[2] Julius Müller, *Die Christliche Lehre von der Sünde*, vol. i., p. 169.

[3] Manu and Zoroaster among them.

word as well as of deed : but Christ, like conscience, condemns evil *motives*, and not merely or primarily their results. It is not only *sins*, but *sin*, from which man needs deliverance, since sin is moral leprosy as well as rebellion and lawlessness. Hence Christianity does not strive to lay down regulations for the control of evil passions ; it condemns these evil desires to death. It has " substituted a principle of life for a code of rules," as Lightfoot says. " Philosophy hopes to cure the vices of human nature by working upon the head, and Christianity by educating the heart," [1] as Aristotle very, very dimly seemed almost to see to be the only possible way to succeed. " Philosophy undertakes to explain what it is right to do, while Christianity undertakes to make men disposed to do it." The world needs a system, not of ethics, but of dynamics. All philosophies and all other religions fail, and have always failed, because they lack " the dynamics of morality." [2] Nothing but the " dynamite " of love to God could lift the fallen and burst the walls of their dungeon. Nor could it be produced in the human heart except in one way. " Herein is love ; not that we loved God, but that He loved us, and sent His Son to be the propitiation for our sins. We love Him, because He first loved us." This is fact, not fiction, as many of us know. It is this that has already in some manner changed the ancient into the modern conception of ethics, that has given us new views regarding our duty to God and our fellow men, the meaning and value of life, the nature of the salvation which men need, the object of prayer. It is this fact of God's love to man revealed in Christ's life, death and

---

[1] Sir John Seeley, *Ecce Homo*.   [2] Archdeacon Moule.

resurrection, that has made " the law of liberty "
take the place of the moral codes of the past. The
" Man of Sorrows " has, by His very existence, rendered
sorrow bearable and suffering in some degree intelligible,[1]
while His atonement assures us of pardon, if we will seek
it, and of " grace to help in time of need." All the
experience of nearly nineteen centuries has proved that
He Who " came to seek and to save that which was lost "
is able to raise the fallen and to change despair and
remorse into repentance and peace with God. Thus
Christ has substituted the positive for the negative in
morals, and altered the prohibition of doing evil into
the command to us to do good, following His example,
" Who went about doing good." That motive-power
which all the learning and wisdom of the world had not
been able to supply has ever since flowed forth from
Christ, giving life and energy to the dead and helpless,
though noble, sentiments and aspirations of the past,
and inspiring humanity with a new and lively hope
through the knowledge of a Heavenly Father and of His
Holiness, Mercy, and Love, manifested in His Son, Jesus
Christ our Lord.

[1] " As love multiplies, suffering must multiply, too. The
very heart of God is full of infinite, joyful, hopeful suffering ; the
whole thing is so vast, so slow, so quiet, that the end of suffering is
yet far off. But, when we suffer, we climb fast ; the spirit grows
old and wise in faith and love ; and suffering is the one thing we
cannot dispense with, because it is the condition of our fullest
and purest life."—A. C. Benson, *The Child of the Dawn*, p. 25.

CHAPTER XIII

Prayer

THE impulse which bids men pray is instinctive and universal, though capable of being resisted. Prayers vary very much in character and aim. A man's prayer may justly be said to be, if genuine, the mirror of his character. Thus the Ṭhags of India used to pray to their bloodthirsty goddess, Kâlî, to give them craft enough to entrap unwary travellers and strangle them as an offering to her, while the booty would supply their own needs. In ancient times at least, the vengeful man would often pray to the dread Powers of Darkness that injury might befall his enemy. An instance of this occurs in the much misunderstood Psalm cix, where the Psalmist appeals unto God to preserve him from the evil plots of his enemies, and quotes the following prayer which they, he says, are using against him :—

> Set Thou a wicked man over him :
> And let an adversary stand at his right hand.
> When he is judged, let him come forth guilty ;
> And let his prayer be turned into sin.
> Let his days be few ;
> And let another take his office.
> Let his children be fatherless,
> And his wife a widow.
> Let his children be vagabonds, and beg ;
> And let them seek their bread out of their desolate places.

Let the extortioner catch all that he hath ;
And let strangers make spoil of his labour.
Let there be none to extend mercy unto him ;
Neither let there be any to have pity on his fatherless children,
    etc.

In conjunction with prayers such as this, incantations
and "black magic" were often used; including such
practices as those carried on in Babylon of old and thence
introduced into Europe by the Canidias of ancient Rome
and the Medeas and other worshippers of Hecate in the
Grecian world, and afterwards prevalent among witches
and wizards in the Middle Ages. Such people seem not
seldom to have been hired by wicked princes to destroy
their private enemies by forming waxen images of them
and melting these before the fire, in the confident belief
that the person thus represented would in the same
manner slowly waste away. Among Assyrian religious
texts we find a prayer to the Fire-god, Gishbar, in which
the petitioner entreats him to preserve him from such
devices and to destroy those who are so wickedly plotting
against him. A few extracts suffice to show what such
a petition was like :—

O mighty Gishbar, raging storm,
Thou dost guide aright gods and princes,
Thou judgest the judgment of male and female destroyer.
In my judgment blaze like the warlike Sun-god,
Judge my judgment, decree the decree,
Burn up the wizard and the witch.
Eat up my foes, forsake mine enemies :
Let thy violent storm overcome them.

*   *   *   *

Let them die, and let me live :
Let them pass away, and let me flourish :
Let them perish, and let me abide :
Let them grow weak, and let me be strong.

O Gishbar the brilliant, exalted one of the gods,
Conqueror of the enemy and of the foe, conquer them, and let me
   not be destroyed.
I am thy servant : let me live, let me be safe, and let me stand
   firm before thee.[1]

Dr. Tylor quotes the following as specimens of the prayers of modern barbarians, in which the prayer is accompanied with a sacrifice, in virtue of which the worshipper begs from his god or gods a recompense of the good things of the earth. [2] " Thus, among the Zulus, the sacrificer says : ' There is your bullock, ye spirits of our people. I pray for a healthy body that I may live comfortably, and thou, So-and-so, treat me with mercy, and thou, So-and-So ' (mentioning by name the dead of the family). The following is part of a prayer of the Khonds, when offering a human sacrifice to the Earth-goddess : ' By our cattle, our flocks, our pigs and our grain we procured a victim and offered a sacrifice. Do you now enrich us. Let our herds be so numerous that they cannot be housed ; let children so abound that the care of them shall be too much for the parents, as shall be seen by their burnt hands ; let our heads ever strike against brass pots innumerable hanging from our roofs ; let the rats form their nests of shreds of scarlet cloth and silk ; let all the kites in the country be seen in the trees of our village, from beasts being killed there every day. We are ignorant of what it is good to ask for. You know what is good for us. Give it to us.' "
Some of the prayers in the Egyptian *Book of the Dead* are interesting, and not a few passages in the Hymns

[1] Martin's *Textes Religeux assyriens et babyloniens*, 1st series, pp. 140 and 146.
[2] *Anthropology*, p. 365.

to the Sun-god in the same work are full of lofty poetry,
and perhaps of true religious feeling. The same thing
may be said of some of the prayers of the Assyrians and
Babylonians. In fact, prayer must first of all be believing and earnest before it can become lifeless and formal.
One of Nebuchadnezzar's prayers to Marduk may be
quoted here[1] :—

" O Prince, thou art from everlasting, lord of all that
exists, for the king whom thou lovest, whom thou callest
by name, as it seems good unto thee thou guidest his
name aright, thou watchest over him in the path of
righteousness. I, the prince who obeys thee, am the
work of thy hands ; thou hast created me, and hast
entrusted to me the sovereignty over multitudes of
men, according to thy goodness, O lord, which thou hast
made to pass over them all. Let me love thy supreme
lordship, let the fear of thy divinity exist in my heart,
and give what seemeth good unto thee, since thou main-
tainest my life."

In the *Rig-Veda* we find men praying mostly for
cattle and wealth, victory over their enemies and abundance of the good things of this world. But occasionally
a deeper note is struck, as in Vasishtha's prayer to
Varuṇa, when the petitioner is afflicted with illness and
is convinced that this is a punishment sent upon him
by Varuṇa for a sin of which he is well aware.

> I ask, O Varuṇa, my guilt perceiving,
> I go the wise, the well-informed, to question.
> They all with one accord at once give answer,
> "'Tis Varuṇa who is incensed against thee."

*　　*　　*　　*

[1] Sayce's translation, *Religions of Ancient Egypt and Babylonia,* p. 323.

'Twas not, O Varuna, my will ; 'twas folly,
Outburst of passion, drunkenness or madness,
An old man overcome by youthful passion,
Nay, sleep or sloth are oft-times cause of sinning.

But as a slave will I now serve the gracious,
And, freed from guilt, obey the jealous Godhead.
A fool who trusts in him learns from him wisdom ;
He, the All-Wise, gives to the prudent riches.

O may this hymn of mine, thou mighty Ruler,
Touch thy kind heart, O Varuna, dear master.
Ye gods, be with us working or reposing,
And shield us ever with all heavenly blessings.[1]

The writer of this hymn had been a devotee of Indra during his youth, as that deity bestowed wealth and power and favoured drunkenness. But here in sickness he feels his guilt and his need of a more spiritual and more moral deity. Hence he " turns at once to the old loving deity, the only maintainer of righteousness, the Being who alone cares for the moral well-being of man, who punishes guilt, who alone can and will pardon the penitent."

As an example of a prayer of quite a different kind, we quote the famous Gâyatrî (also called Sâvitrî), which every Hindû still repeats at dawn in the very same Sanskrit tongue in which it has been repeated ever since Vedic times. It has prefixed to it the sacrosanct syllables *Ôm bhûr bhavaḥ suvaḥ ôm*, the meaning of which is almost lost in the mist of ages, though the first and last word probably at one time signified something like " Amen," and the others most likely denote " Earth, air, sky." Then comes the prayer itself, addressed to the Sun-god :

[1] *Rig-Veda*, vii., 86 ; from Canon Cook's *Origins of Religion and Language*, pp. 48, 49.

" We meditate on that excellent brightness of the Sun-god ; and may he prosper our prayers."

Among the Zoroastrians of India there are three famous prayers, also very ancient, one of which begins with the words *Yathâ Ahû Vairyô*. It may be thus rendered :—

" As a Lord should be chosen, so should a priest for justification, as giver of a good disposition, of deeds of life (pleasing) to Mazda (and to Ahura belongs the sover-eignty), whom let him give as a protector to the poor." This formula is constantly on the lips of the pious Pârsî, and it is repeated again and again in the religious cere-monies of that faith. The Avesta assures us that by repeating it Zoroaster repelled the Evil Spirit (*drukhsh*) which Ahriman had sent flying from the North to destroy the prophet.

As deep religious feeling dies away and men's thoughts turn more and more to worldly things, prayer loses its vitality and tends to become a mass of vain repetitions. Thus in India the pious Hindû earns merit for himself by repeating hundreds of times the name " Râm, Râm," or " Hari, Hari," according to whether he is a devotee of Râma or Vishṇu. Similarly the Muslim stores up merit by repeating the word *Allâh* (God) over and over again, or by reciting certain verses of the Qur'ân, or by getting the whole of it read aloud in Arabic, of which he need not understand a word. So the Sikhs repeat their Jap-jî, and the Lamaists turn their prayer-wheels. The " vain repetitions " so dear to the heathen are not altogether unknown in certain branches of the Christian Church: witness the origin of such words as " patter " (from " Pater noster ") and a few others. It is very remarkable how sacred dead languages become in the minds of men whose religion is also dead or dying. Witness the practices of the Muslims, Jews, Armenians, Russians, Copts and Abyssinians, who use Arabic, Hebrew, ancient Armenian, Old Slavonic, Coptic and Æthiopic respectively in their regular services, all the more fervently because they do not understand them. Prayers no longer understood become sacred mysteries, charms, talismans, magic formulæ of wondrous efficacy, whose power it is impious to doubt. In fact, they may ultimately become potent enough to force the gods to do what the worshipper desires, as in the case of the *Karakia* of the heathen Maoris and the *mantra* of the Hindûs. The first sign of real spiritual life is when a man, forgetting or neglecting such ancient and now all but unmeaning formulas, turns to God and pours forth in his native tongue a prayer straight from his heart.

In this matter of prayer, Christianity introduced into the ancient world of Jews and Gentiles as great a change, and wrought as stupendous a spiritual revolution, as it does now when the Gospel is preached for the first time in the dark places of the earth. As Fustel de Coulanges well says [1] : " Christianity changed the nature and the form of worship. Man no longer gave to God food and drink : prayer was no longer a formula of incantation, it was an act of faith and a humble petition. The spirit was in a different relation to the Deity : the fear of the gods was replaced by the Love of God." The Polish writer, Senkovich, also thus describes the effect which the spectacle of Christian worship, seen for the first time, had upon a noble Roman of Nero's reign :—

" In Asia Minor, in Egypt, and in Rome itself, Vinitius had seen a multitude of very different kinds of temples ; he had acquainted himself with a multitude of different

[1] *La Cité antique*, p. 487.

religions, and had heard a multitude of canticles. But now, for the first time, did he see people invoking with a hymn a Deity, not for the fulfilment of some established ritual, but from a pure heart, with such longing for this Deity as children might cherish for their father or mother. One must be blind not to perceive that these people not only adored their God but also loved Him with their whole soul ; and Vinitius had not hitherto seen this, whether in any country or at any ceremonies or in any temples. In Rome and Greece, those who still paid honour to their gods did so from fear, or from the desire to make sure of their assistance, but to no one did it even occur to love them." [1] This is hardly to be wondered at when we consider the character and conduct of these deities. They were conceived of as more than human in their vices, less than human in their virtues. Lucretius well says of heathenism :

Religio peperit scelerosa atque impia facta

and gives as an example the way in which " the chosen leaders of the Danaï " shed the blood of Iphigenia on the altar of Artemis to appease the goddess and to secure a favourable breeze to carry them to Troy. Bad as such deities were, they might, it was held, be moved by prayer, sacrifice, and sacred rite, to pity and help men in their distress. But the gods of the philosopher himself were, though less immoral, still worse and less likely to help, since he thus describes them in accordance with the Epicurean philosophy which he held :—

For all the gods by nature surely must
In deepest peace immortal life enjoy,

---

[1] *Quo Vadis* ? Pt. i., ch. xx., Russian version.

> From human cares and troubles far remote :
> From sorrow free, to dangers ne'er exposed,
> Rich in themselves and needing nought of ours,
> Virtues they heed not, nor with anger burn.

In contrast with both conceptions of the gods, Christianity told of the " Man of Sorrows," Who, being One with the Heavenly Father, revealed Him in His Holiness, Justice, and Love.

True worship is not mere asking, nor even adoration and praise. Our Lord tells us that the condition of its acceptance is that it be " in spirit and in truth," and that the Father seeks such worshippers. It is needless to say that the Christian worshipper does not desire to change the All-Loving and All-Wise Father's will, but rather to be brought into thorough and conscious harmony with it. This is evident from the model prayer our Lord taught us, incorporating into it all that was best of the current petitions [1] of the Jewish people, and yet adding to them and perfecting them into one perfect whole. Prayer is communion with God. This and all other spiritual activities " seem to arise from man's consciousness that when he is most alone . . . he is in company with another spirit, and can have distinct dealings with that other, dealings which we may describe by the new word ' telepathic,' for that is the only word that expresses the communion of two intelligences without sensuous medium." [2] Even with prayer it is

---

[1] There is good reason to believe that certain of the petitions in the Lord's Prayer were in use among the Jews in His time. Yet they have never yet so united them as to include in any of their Prayer Books a prayer at all comparable with that which Christ taught.

[2] *Voluntas Dei*, p. 92.

sometimes hard enough to get through life and to do one's duty. Without prayer, many men find it impossible. But what is needed is to *pray*, not merely to say prayers, for between the two there is the same difference as between a living man and a corpse.

> Touch but the skirt of God when thou dost pray,
> And He shall hold thy hand through all the day.[1]

The late Mr. Moncure D. Conway says[2] that there is a great tendency at the present day for prayer to grow formal and unreal, through discussions about the " First Cause," which one cannot well worship. But he indicates the only possible cure for this atrophy of the spiritual faculties when he adds :—

All that is mystical or poetic in the universe draws near to us only in that Face. For multitudes, their life-journey is nearly all through a dark vale ; and when the weary wayfarer hears in his dream a voice of early faith, saying, " Seek thou My face," his heart replies, " Thy face, Lord, will I seek ! " There can be no love nor prayer where there is no face. Never did heartfelt prayer ascend to the Unknowable. We ascribe faces to abstractions— charity, justice, truth, mercy—longing to give objective reality to qualities and sentiments we revere. But the source of prayer is deeper than reverence ; it is love : and in the personified Beloved is imaged every face—of child, parent, lover, friend—that ever smiled upon that kneeling spirit, to be shaped at last in that Face which lightens the Dark Vale with devotion and tenderness.

---

[1] Langbridge.   [2] In the *North American Review*.

CHAPTER XIV

God and Man

THAT there is some relation between God and man is a belief which underlies religion in general and every form of worship. But what that relation is has been a matter in which religions have never yet agreed. Those who have lost all conception of a Deity higher than their own deceased ancestors naturally claim descent from these " gods," if such they can be called. Similarly, in ancient Egypt the Pharaohs, and in modern Japan the Mikados, claim descent from the Sun-god for themselves. The Incas of Peru made the same claim. But in such cases this Divine descent was supposed to be peculiar to the monarchs, and not to belong to their subjects. Elsewhere very commonly it has been held that one or more of the gods—Khnum in Egypt, Merodach and the goddess Aruru in Babylonia, Pachacamac among the Peruvians—made man, and that the relation between God and man is therefore that between Creator and creature, the potter and the vessel which he has turned and shaped on his wheel. Sometimes it has been thought that this gave the Deity some interest in His creatures ; at other times it was considered as giving Him an absolute right to do with them as He would, while denying them any claim upon Him for kindness, mercy, or justice.

A very prevalent idea in many religions always has

been that a certain degree of likeness exists between the
gods and men. In many cases this likeness is such that
the gods have material bodies, as men have. Not unfrequently these bodies are in human form, though at times
they are like certain animals : or the gods assume any
form they please. Whether they have human forms
or not, the deities are generally regarded as having human
passions. The idea of One Holy God is found nowhere
except among Jews and Christians. Even among the
Zoroastrians of old, Ahura-Mazdâ's spouse was his own
daughter Ârmaiti. Among the Hindûs of Vedic times
Indra is accused of many crimes, the least serious of
them being drunkenness. In one of the Purânas, Brahmâ
is accused of a guilty passion for Vâch, his daughter.
The conduct of Zeus and other gods among the Greeks
is well known. The likeness which such religions as
these hold to exist between the gods and men lies in the
fact that men have made for themselves gods in their
own immoral image. We have already said, but the
fact cannot be too often insisted on, that nowhere but
in Judaism and Christianity is the conception of God's
Holiness entertained : hence these evil passions which
have so long swayed men's hearts and lives have been
considered as characteristic of their deities too. The
reflex effect of such an idea has been terrible. Men have
justified their own evil deeds by the example of their
gods, and have even deemed themselves the special
favourites of certain deities because they indulged in
the crimes which were regarded as particularly under
those gods' patronage. Thus at Rome, Mercury was the
god of thieves ; in Hellas, Hecatê presided over witchcraft
and poisoning ; in Phrygia, Cybele patronized impurity ;
in India, Durgâ encouraged murder.

Hindûism considers that gods and men are closely related to one another, not only because in their vices they are much alike, but also because gods, demons, men, animals and all things that exist are all parts of the One Thing. Even when not so fully developed, their Pantheism leads to the idea that the Deity is the source of all things, and that into It all things will be ultimately absorbed, men thus entirely losing whatever personality they may now have. This is, in fact, the Hindû idea of salvation (*moksha*, *mukti*). Pantheism is essentially immoral. In Greece and Rome the Stoic philosophy also rested upon belief in Pantheism, although the language which some of its most eloquent exponents often used regarding God shows that the religious instinct, or the " light that lighteth every man coming into the world," made them at times feel the great truth of God's personality and of their dependence on Him. Thus Seneca asks, " What is God ? " and replies, " The mind of the Universe, . . . all that you see and all that you do not see." Yet he speaks of Him as personal, and asks, " Does not God bestow kindnesses ? Whence then are those things which you possess ? " In answer to the statement that Nature gives all this, he says, " Do you not understand that, when you say this, you are changing a name for God ? For what is Nature but God and the divine reason inserted into the whole world and its parts ? " The Stoics often preferred to speak of God in this sense by the old name of Zeus. Hence [1] Aratos (about 270 B.C.) says, " Everywhere we have all need of Zeus, for his very offspring are we." St. Paul [2] (as

---

[1] *Phaenomena*, near beginning. So Cleanthes, 300 B.C., addressing Zeus, says, " for from thee are we an offspring."

[2] Acts xvii. 28.

we have seen) quotes the latter words, recognizing and making full and frank use of the truth which they contain. He thus sets us an example of the use which may wisely be made of the facts on which the science of Comparative Religion rests.

It is worthy of note that Ṣûfî philosophy, in its revolt from " orthodox " Islâm, has reached the same belief in man's filial relationship to God. Islâm itself teaches that there is no such relation. He is our absolute Master and we are His slaves. God's decree is fate. He decreed every man's eternal happiness or misery ages before the creation of the world, without a thought of mercy or pity. In the Qur'ân He is represented as saying, " Verily [1] I will fill Hell with genii and men all together," and as declaring that He had created them for this purpose.[2] So in a tradition Muḥammad says that God showed Adam the spirits of his yet unborn descendants, and then divided them into two parties, placing one on the right and the other on the left. Of those on the right hand He said, " These are for Paradise, and I care not." Then, turning to those on the left, He said, " These are for Hell fire, and I care not."[3] God is called the Merciful, the Just, the Loving, and by many other lofty titles ; but it is taught that what are called mercy, justice and love in God bear no resemblance to the attributes which have the same names in man, because there is no likeness whatever between God and man, the Creator and His creature. Maimonides, among the Jewish philosophers of the Middle Ages, uses language very similar on this latter point, as has already been said.

[1] Sûrahs xi., 120, and xxxii., 13.
[2] Sûrah xi., 120, and vii., 178.   [3] *Mishkât*, pp. 15 and 16.

Such a conclusion necessarily follows from any system of barren Monotheism.

But there is a tradition, authentic or not, that Muhammed himself once used the expression, " Mankind are God's family ; therefore he who does good unto His family is dearest to God." The Ṣûfîs have gladly availed themselves of this phrase and made all that they could of the truth which it contains. But here again the essential Pantheism of that system of philosophy has largely hindered such a saying from producing its proper result.

Amid all the animal-worship of ancient Egypt it is cheering to find certain great truths at times asserting themselves. Thus Paul Pierret quotes the saying *Ar rethu šennu n Nuther*, " Man is God's second (*or* ' comrade,' ' like ')." In the *Asclepius*, attributed to Apuleius, something similar occurs. In that book the Egyptian deity, Thoth, is represented as teaching that God, the Lord of eternity, has two images of Himself, the first being the world, and the second man. Man is partly divine and partly mundane ; his soul, feeling, spirit and reason being in their nature divine, but his body being made of the elements fire, water and air, and therefore earthly and mortal.

This likeness between God and man in certain respects was admitted by some of the poets and philosophers of Greece and Rome. Euripides declares that the human mind is God ; Cicero says that it is like God, because to remember, be wise, invent, are divine things. It was argued that the human mind could not be accounted for by any material cause or origin, and that it must, therefore, in its very nature be divine. Seneca asserts that the possession of a mind unites man, as such, with

God, whether the man be a Roman knight, a freedman, or a slave. In this he recognized the existence of a relationship between God and man, as did Cleanthes and others of the same school, though agreeing with Plato that one could not know God properly. Juvenal rightly sees in human sympathy something divine. Cicero urges that, as man alone has a knowledge of God's existence and is naturally led to worship Him, this is a great proof of his immortality and of his affinity with God.

Thus, in religion after religion, and in philosophical schools belonging to different ages and countries, we find more or less consciousness of the fact that there is some relationship, some resemblance, been God and man. In many instances this conviction has been abused, as we have seen ; for in ancient times, as in the present, may be found " wretched and evil men, whose yearnings are downward to the darkness, instead of heavenward, and who, could they but extinguish the lights which God has kindled for us, would count the midnight gloom their chiefest glory." [1] Yet we naturally look for any lofty views which men have entertained, though unable to shut our eyes to others : and what we find is an inkling of the truth rather than an apprehension of it. " What is truth ? " was often asked in many lands before Christ came ; but no certain answer could be returned. Men had to content themselves, as Plato says, with the most unanswerable of human reasonings, hoping for some Word of God to bear them, as on a raft, across the ocean of uncertainty. At last " the Word was made flesh and dwelt among us, and we beheld His glory."

Quite early in the Bible the grand fact is revealed that

[1] Nathaniel Hawthorne.

man is made in God's image, after His likeness. Marred as it has been by sin, that likeness has never been obliterated. The lost piece of money still bears the Sovereign's image and superscription, and its Owner will seek for it until He find it. But man's likeness to God does not consist wholly, or even chiefly (as philosophers fancied), in man's intellect. The spiritual faculties are higher than the mental, and so it is the spiritual and not the psychical man who can know the things of God Who is a Spirit. Only the pure in heart can see God. Men are God's creatures, all of whom He loves ; and He longs to make them His children, to give them the right to become sons of God, to give them the new spiritual birth from above, in His Son Jesus Christ. " Behold what manner of love the Father hath bestowed upon us, that we should be called children of God : and such we are. . . . . Beloved, now are we children of God, and it is not yet made manifest what we shall be. We know that, if He shall be manifested, we shall be like Him, for we shall see Him even as He is. And every one that hath this hope set on Him purifieth himself, even as He is pure."[1] Children, as such, should grow ; and so Christians should " grow in the grace and knowledge of our Lord and Saviour Jesus Christ," " till we all attain unto the unity of the faith and of the knowledge of the Son of God, unto a full-grown man, unto the measure of the stature of the fulness of Christ." Such is the Christian view of the relation between God and man.

Among the children of God [says Ruskin], there is always that fearful and bowed apprehension of His majesty, and that sacred dread of all offence to Him, which is called the fear of God. Yet

---

[1] 1 John iii. 1–3.

of real and essential fear there is not any, but clinging of confidence to Him as their Rock, Fortress and Deliverer ; and perfect love, and casting out of fear. So it is not possible that, while the mind is rightly bent on Him, there should be dread of anything earthly or supernatural. And the more dreadful seems the height of His majesty, the less fear they feel that dwell in the shadow of it.

According to the Gospel, we are called to be workers together with God, helping in the accomplishment of His " purpose of the ages." Yet His service is perfect freedom and we are given complete freewill.

> Our wills are ours, we know not how ;
> Our wills are ours, to make them Thine.

Our personality, being one of God's choicest gifts, will never be taken back from us. There is no absorption into the Deity like that of the raindrop lost in the ocean from which it came. Yet there will be unity and harmony of will and aim and work. " His servants shall do Him service ; and they shall see His face ; and His Name shall be on their foreheads."

CHAPTER XV

Duty to our Neighbour

IN olden times, among all nations, every one who did not belong to one's own nation or tribe—or even to one's own city or village—was regarded as an enemy, and as such had no recognized rights. None of the religions of the heathen world disputed this fact, or taught that a man owed any duty at all to other men, as such, though he might owe something to them as members of the same state. " Not till the word ' barbarian ' was struck out of the dictionary of mankind and replaced by ' brother,' not till the right of all nations of the world to be classed as members of one genus or kind was recognized," as Max Müller has pointed out, was it possible for men even to consider the connexion between languages of the same stock, much less that between different races of men. " This change was effected by Christianity. To the Hindû every man not ' twice-born ' was a *Mlechchha*, to the Greek every man not speaking Greek was a barbarian, to the Jew every person not circumcised was a Gentile. . . . It was Christianity which first broke down the barriers between Jew and Gentile, between Greek and Barbarian, between the white and the black. ' Humanity ' is a word which you look for in vain in Plato or Aristotle : the idea of mankind as one family, as the children of one

God, is an idea of Christian growth." [1] It is true that
here and there the thought did now and then occur to
one or two specially favoured individuals that there was
some common bond of nature between men as such, but
these instances are so few that it would not be difficult
to count them all. In Latin literature Terence's saying
is almost unique : " I am a man : nothing human do I
deem alien to me." Somewhat similar in meaning is the
saying supposed to have been uttered by Buddha in a
previous life : " Through addiction to one's own pleasure,
or from loss of strength, another's pain is overlooked ;
and while another's pain exists there is no pleasure for
me ; and while I have strength how am I to be indifferent ? " [2] But these rare exceptions serve only to prove
the rule and to cause the general apathy to stand out in
clearer relief.

Even within the same state or religious community all
men had by no means the same right to justice and consideration. The immense masses of slaves in the Roman
Empire had no rights at all. They were on the same footing as their masters' cattle. In all religions except the
Christian (and in a measure the Jewish), the position of
women [3] was very low, not least so in Greece. So it is
under all non-Christian faiths to the present day, unless
it be considered socially higher (though morally lower)
where polyandry prevails, as among the Nairs of India.
Even to-day Islâm permits polygamy, unlimited freedom
of divorce, and servile concubinage, with all their attendant
evils. Family life under such conditions can hardly be

---

[1] Pliny, iii., 3, is no real contradiction to this.
[2] *Jâtaka-Mâlâ*, i., šl. 23.
[3] Vide Gun's *Christianity and Woman*, passim.

said to have any true existence. Buddhism, as taught by its founder, prohibited marriage to all members of the Order (*Sangho*), male and female. Only " lay adherents " might marry, not true Buddhists. Belief that all suffering is the penalty or " fruit " of evil-doing in this or in some previous existence very largely destroys all sympathy with the sufferer in all lands where Buddhism prevails, as also among Hindûs. Among the latter the caste system has the same effect. Thus duty to one's neighbour has never, apart from Christianity, been felt to be a thing specially important to perform. The tendency was generally not even to ask, " Who is my neighbour, and to whom am I under any obligation whatever to show kindness ? " but rather to repudiate all duty, except within very narrow limits, to one's fellow-men.

It is true, as has been said, that noble sentiments, and occasionally noble actions, are to be found in the literature of non-Christian nations. The ancient Egyptian, in inscriptions within his tomb, not rarely boasts that he has given bread to the hungry and clothed the naked. These actions are undertaken in the East at the present day to some extent, but almost wholly (not because of any feeling of duty, but) in order to acquire merit for oneself, which may cause the doer to escape the punishment of his sins. It is with the purpose of securing an acquittal at Osiris' judgment-seat that the dead in ancient Egypt are represented as setting forth their own good deeds of this kind : and this fact shows that they did not recognize it as a duty which they had discharged, but as a work of supererogation. Buddhism commanded men to feel sympathy with and to entertain sentiments of *benevolence* towards all beings, but not to indulge in *beneficence*. Confucius inculcates the duty of revenge.

He also urges that evil should be recompensed with evil, good with good. This is the popular saying prevalent as a rule of ethics, in one form or another, in many lands : " Thou shalt love thy neighbour, and hate thine enemy." *In a negative form* the Golden Rule has been found in Greece, India and China : " Do not unto another what you would not wish him to do to you." In the *Tao-teh-Kying*, however—a work ascribed to Laou-tsze—the positive form of the injunction, " Recompense injury with kindness," occurs. A work, entitled *Kan-ying-p'ien* (" Rewards and Punishments "), belonging to the fifteenth century of the Christian era, contains not a few noble sentiments : but of it has been said by one who has passed the larger part of his life in China, " This book, which strongly sways the moral thoughts of the people, lacks that which Confucius and Mencius learned to their sorrow was lacking in their own teaching—the dynamics of morality, the power to do the good and refuse the evil." [1] As Laou-tsze recognized no personal God, it is hardly to be wondered at that he could not supply any adequate motive power to enable men to do what he advised, though even such a recognition is generally inadequate to that effect.

It is well known that our Lord not only gave the Golden Rule in its *positive* form, " Whatsoever ye would that men should do you, do ye even so to them," and combined with it such precepts as " Love your enemies" and those which inculcate the duty of forgiveness " unto seventy times seven," but that He also *carried His principles into practice*—a useful thing in this practical world. He also gave His disciples the will and the power to imitate Him in this respect, and thus to make His precepts

[1] *Splendour of a Great Hope*, p. 101.

not dead rules but living principles of action in the life and work of every day. His prayer, " Father, forgive them, for they know not what they do," led St. Stephen to pray " Lord, lay not this sin to their charge." The " Good Samaritan " remained no longer a character in a parable, but became a person who might be seen at work wherever Christians were found, and who lives and works to-day in every land.

To take only one example : there were no hospitals before Christianity arose, certainly not among Buddhists,[1] as has been rashly asserted. The first hospitals known in history were those erected at Rome and Ostia by a Christian lady named Fabiola. This was a practical way of acting the Good Samaritan, and one which has been followed up ever since. Christianity in its outward manifestation consists in the " Imitation of Christ," Who went about doing good. It is essentially practical, not merely theoretical : and, in the actual world of sin and sorrow in which our lot is cast, something more than theory is needed. Hence it is that " the sinner whom Christ habitually denounces is he *who has done nothing.*"[2]

---

[1] Ašoka's Second Edict contains the word *chikisakâ*, which Bühler translated " Hospitals," but wrongly. It is probably the plural of the Sanskṛit word *chikitsaka*, " physician," or possibly a derivative of Sanskṛit *chikitsâ*, " cure, healing " ; from the root *kit* (cf. *chit* 4), " to cure." [In Pâli from the same root we have *tikichchhako*, " physician," and *tikichchhâ*, " cure."] In neither Pâli nor Sanskṛit is there any word for " hospital." The context in the Edict would not suit hospitals, as is well shown in Mr. Howard Nash's *Pagan and Christian Parallels*, pp. 49, 50. Some have stated that the Spaniards found hospitals in Mexico when they landed. If there is any truth in the statement, they may have been due to Quetzalcoatl, who can hardly have been other than a European Christian.

[2] *Ecce Homo*, Dent's Ed., p. 149.

One point, therefore, in which Christianity showed itself to be a new influence in the world when it first appeared, and very different from other religions, was that it gave a motive and a permanent impulse to every kind of positive goodness. When it ceases to exercise this influence, the salt will have lost its savour, and will be fit for nothing but to be cast forth and trodden under foot of men.

" Christ believed it possible to bind men to their kind, but on one condition—that they were first bound fast to Himself. He stood forth as the representative of men, He identified Himself with the cause and with the interests of all human beings, He was destined . . . to lay down His life for them. Few of us sympathize originally and directly with this devotion ; few of us can perceive in human nature itself any merit sufficient to evoke it. But it is not so hard to love and venerate Him who felt it. So vast a passion of love, a devotion so comprehensive, elevated, deliberate and profound, has not elsewhere been in any degree approached save by some of His imitators. And as love provokes love, many have found it possible to conceive for Christ an attachment the closeness of which no words can describe, a veneration so possessing and absorbing the man within them that they have said, ' I live no more, but Christ lives in me.' Now such a feeling carries with it of necessity the feeling of love for all human beings." [1] Thus Christ taught and still teaches our duty to our neighbour, giving that word, originally so limited in its meaning, a significance as wide as the human race itself.

[1] *Ecce Homo*, p. 133.

P

CHAPTER XVI

Conclusion

FROM our investigations in the preceding chapters it is evident that there are certain great matters upon which, in their general outline though not in details, all religions may be said to agree in the main. Among the chief of these are : (*a*) the existence of a Deity or deities, (*b*) the fact that there is an After-life of some kind, and (*c*) that worship is not in vain. Besides this, not a few religions also recognize : (*d*) the need of a Saviour or deliverer, (*e*) the distinction between good and evil, and (*f*) the final triumph of the good.

On Aristotle's principle that the general agreement of mankind upon a question proves its truth, we may at least draw the inference that much of the religious system of which this is a faint outline, and which in a measure seems to underlie all human religions, is true.

How then does Christianity stand with regard to these great and vital points in what a few generations ago would have been called " Natural Religion " ? What further light does the Gospel throw upon the problems involved in them, and what does it do to dispel the mistiness with which they are put forth by various Ethnic faiths ?

Christianity accepts and teaches every one of these great

doctrines, but elevates each of them to an infinitely higher level than does any other creed.

The Bible does not merely teach the existence of God, but also His Personality, Unity, Holiness, Justice, Mercy, Love, and other Divine Attributes. Avoiding the polytheism of so many faiths and their degradation of the conception of the Divine, the Pantheism of Hindûism, the barren Monotheism of Islâm, and Jewish philosophy, Christianity teaches God's Transcendence and at the same time His Immanence.

The doctrine of the Trinity in Unity explains how it is possible for God to reveal Himself in Christ so as to be really known to His creatures, thus satisfying the impulse that, when abused, leads to Idolatry, and showing the truth of the instinct in which originated the Hindû doctrine of *Avatâras*.

The doctrine of Christ's self-sacrifice and Atonement explains and justifies the sacrificial[1] instinct found among all nations, while it teaches us our reasonable duty to become in Him " living sacrifices, holy, acceptable to God." Christianity reveals a Saviour Whose worthiness and power " to save to the uttermost all that come unto God through Him " the Gospel, together with all history since His time, abundantly proves.

It brings to light a future existence of " life and incorruption," of living and loving service to God, of holiness, of happiness undefiled and that passeth not away.

Its Ethics are the highest conceivable, aiming at perfection, and laying down eternal *principles*, not formal rules.

Lastly, Christ's love supplies the mightiest and most

[1] Vide the chapter on Sacrifice in my *Comparative Religion* (Longmans).

unselfish motive-power that can be conceived of, thus giving men that without which no system of morals would aught avail, and for lack of which men's highest philosophies and loftiest aspirations had always and everywhere previously failed to attain their aim.

Looking at the matter from this point of view, it may be said that, if we liken the religious outlines above mentioned to a faint sketch left unfinished by the painter and somewhat blurred and rendered indistinct by the efforts to complete it made by many daubers since, Christianity may be compared with the finished picture by a master's hand. The perfectness of the completion shows that it has been done by one who has thoroughly grasped the artist's original plan and entered into his spirit. Or is the first hand the final hand too? Has the Divine Artist Himself, in the fulness of time, filled in His sketch and completed His picture?

Some hold that Christianity is due to a process of evolution in the religious world. According to this theory, religious ideas have gradually developed from ghost-worship, ancestor-worship, and other low forms of belief, slowly growing nobler, purer, worthier, until they have resulted in Christianity. There is something attractive in this view, though, as we shall see, it does not account for all the facts. But if for the present we grant it to be correct, the development or evolution of the spiritual man would be comparable to that of our physical body, on the supposition that the latter has gradually been evolved from lower forms of life. In any case it is admitted that man was the aim of creation from the time of the appearance of the first Palæozoic fishes. As physical man, then, by his process of being evolved, bears evidence to a design and a Designer—God Himself—so the evolution of religion until it has resulted in Christianity must prove that the latter is the accomplishment of a purpose of God—in other words, that it is true and is from God.

There is no doubt that some truth may be found in this theory. But it does not account for all the facts, and therefore cannot be held to be scientifically accurate. The Ptolemaic Theory in Astronomy was for a while accepted, because it at least explained most of the movements of the heavenly bodies observed in early days. But after a time it was found that there were certain great facts for which it could not account, and the theory (in spite of its plausibility) was therefore given up. So in the present case, the evolutionary theory of the origin of Christianity does not account (among other things) for (1) the fact that, wherever we are able to trace any religion back for many ages, we find it purer, nobler, and loftier in its teaching about God in the earliest times than in the latest. This is true of Hindûism, the early religion of China, the primitive faith of the dynastic Egyptians, and in many other instances.

The other fact is (2) that, in the long period which has elapsed since our Lord's life on earth, Evolution ought to have produced still more perfect characters, nobler teachers, holier and better men than He ; or at least it should have made the type normal. It will hardly be contended that this has been so. Whatever truth therefore there may be in the theory, it is not completely satisfactory.

We may, however, concede this much, that the history of religion shows two things : first, man's inability to ascertain the truth for himself, and, secondly, the fact that, in the history of one family and one nation at least,

God had been for ages carrying on the religious education of the human race and working out His gracious purpose, until its culmination in the Jesus of the Evangelists.

It will probably be admitted by most thoughtful men, who have studied the subject, that God as revealed in Christ is the only possible and worthy object of worship in our own day. We cannot adore the man-made " gods " of philosophy ; we cannot return to the worship of Ódhin and Thór, of Zeus and Athene, of Perûn and Stribog. Even those Modernists who deny the actuality of the character and life of Christ, as given by the men who knew and loved Him, yet boldly assert that the " ideal " Christ is the King of a universal kingdom, and that His revelation of God is the only right one. This in our own day proves His claim : " I am the Way, the Truth, and the Life ; no man cometh unto the Father but by Me."

The choice lies between Christianity and Atheism : the former fully accounts for all the facts of Comparative Religion ; the latter gives up the problem as unsolvable.

Some men in our own day assert that the doctrines of Christianity have been derived, consciously or unconsciously, from other and earlier faiths : from India, or from Babylonia, from Egypt or Persia, from Asia Minor or from Greece and Rome, or from all these and many other sources. This assertion they base on a number of more or less close resemblances which they think they can detect between certain Christian tenets and those of some other religions. Resemblances do exist, but often both their number and their details are either totally misrepresented or grossly exaggerated, even by those writers who are too honest to owe their " facts " to their imaginations. Regarding many of these supposed

" parallels " to Christian doctrines in other religions, it
may be said that—

> Mote-like they flutter in unsteady eyes,
> And weakest his who best descries.

Yet, wherever any such resemblances can be really
traced, however faint they may be, they are of the utmost
value and significance, whether we regard them as guesses
at truth, as foreshadowings of what was yet to be fully
revealed, as intuitions of the *Anima humana naturaliter
Christiana* (according to Tertullian's noble phrase), as
relics of an early revelation, as fragments of a sketch
intended for a perfect picture in days to come, or in some
other way.

In previous chapters we have dealt with some of these
alleged resemblances as fully as our space warranted, and
so our readers will be able to judge of their value for
themselves.

One thing is clear : the sketch has been so marred and
torn into such fragments that, but for our now having
the perfect picture, we should never have been able to
put the pieces together or form the least conception of its
original design. Some would have us believe that the
completed portrait is altogether a fancy picture, corresponding to no reality, because some faint likeness to it
may be detected in a few fragments of the supposed original sketch, where the latter is least indistinct. This is
not, we think, the logical conclusion. It seems to us more
probable that the finished portrait and the sketch bear some
resemblance to one another because they both in different
degrees show forth something at least of the glory of the
Supreme Reality of the Truth Himself.

There are two facts [says Professor Sayce [1]] which . . . have been forced upon me by a study of the old religions of civilized humanity. On the one hand, they testify to the continuity of religious thought. God's light lighteth every man that cometh into the world, and the religions of Egypt and Babylonia illustrate the words of the Evangelist. They form, as it were, the background and preparation for Judaism and Christianity. Christianity is the fulfilment, not of the Law only, but of all that was truest and best in the religions of the ancient world. In it the beliefs and aspirations of Egypt and Babylon have found their explanation and fulfilment. But, on the other hand, between Judaism and the coarsely polytheistic religion of Babylonia, as also between Christianity and the old Egyptian faith—in spite of its high morality and spiritual insight—there lies an impassable gulf. And for the existence of this gulf I can find only one explanation, unfashionable and antiquated though it be. In the language of a former generation, it marks the dividing-line between revelation and unrevealed religion.

It has been suggested, doubtless with some degree of truth, that the stories told of Merodach and Osiris, regarding their goodness to men, may in after years, when the Gospel was preached in Babylonia and Egypt, have exerted considerable influence in leading men to accept Christ as being the substance of which those two personifications of the Sun-god were but the shadow. Certainly something of this kind took place in Scandinavia, where the people showed a tendency to identify the "white Christ" with " Baldr the beautiful." Their intuition was correct in so far as it helped them to recognize that the " broken lights," too, were from God, in Whom " is no darkness at all," and that Christ had fulfilled in Himself all the highest hopes of heathendom.

But to say this is quite a different thing from asserting that we Christians, or the Apostles rather, have drawn

---

[1] *Religions of Ancient Egypt and Babylonia*, Preface.

a highly coloured picture of an ideal and unreal Christ based upon what men once believed about Merodach and Osiris, and that, as Jensen [1] ventures to say, we are to-day worshipping " a Babylonian deity." The Sun-god myth,[2] we may safely contend, has been exploded ere this. But that the fables and allegories of the past, as far as they contained any elements of truth, should have been Divinely intended to be, and have been, employed in the service of the Truth is not incredible or even strange.

That the Gospel portraiture of Christ is not a fancy sketch, a romance, a dream, a fable, a " mystery play," a delusion, a story in which the few actual facts have been much or little " embroidered," ought to be clear to any honest man who reads the New Testament. If a man cannot detect the ring of truth in, for example, our Lord's addresses to His disciples and His High-priestly prayer in St. John's Gospel, then no amount of evidence will convince him. The fact that every attempt to prove the late date of the Gospel records by genuine critical investigation has failed, and that the only way in which they can be set aside is by asserting the infallibility of the conclusions drawn by the " inner consciousness " of certain opponents of Christianity, is enough in itself to make earnest men doubt whether it is wise to trust to such men as Bousset (who admits that " we may occasionally make use of our imagination ") in preference to the Apostles.

Canon Ainger [3] has well said—

---

[1] A brief but very effective answer to this and cognate theories is given by Dr. Nuelson in *The Fundamentals*, vol. vi. He shows that exactly the same style of argument would completely resolve Theodore Roosevelt into a mythological figure.

[2] Vide above, pp. 29–34.   [3] *Life*, p. 104.

With eager knife that oft has sliced
A Gentile gloss or Jewish fable,
Before the crowd you lay the Christ
Upon the lecture table.
From bondage to the old beliefs,
You say, our rescue must begin :—
But *I*—want refuge from my griefs,
And saving from my sin.
The strong, the easy and the glad
Hang, blandly listening, on thy word—
But I am sick and I am sad,
And I need Thee, O Lord.

It may safely be said that, with the whole of the world's literature, ancient and modern, now in our hands, we can find nothing in history or romance worthy to be compared with the Gospel portraiture of the Christ. We know well the Ideal Men [1] of all nations, of all philosophies, of all poets ; yet which of them can be even brought forward as His rival ? John Stuart Mill's argument [2] on this point seems conclusive : " Who among His disciples, or among their proselytes, was capable of inventing the sayings ascribed to Jesus, or of imagining the life and character revealed in the Gospels ? Certainly not the fishermen of Galilee ; as certainly not St. Paul, whose character and idiosyncrasies were of a totally different sort ; still less the early Christian writers, in whom nothing is more evident than that the good which was in them was all derived, as they always professed that it was derived, from a higher source." Truth does not spring from falsehood, nor do we owe Him Who is indeed the

[1] See my *Religio Critici*, S.P.C.K., chap. ii., " The Fact of Christ."
[2] Quoted in Sir R. Anderson's *A Doubter's Doubts*, p. 121.

Light of the world to an impious lie. *We have " the Fact of Christ."*

The critical (and the uncritical) world seems nowadays to be more or less obsessed by the Mythical Theory in connexion with Christianity. We hear " the Christus-myth " spoken of as if it had been proved to exist, as if baseless assertion and unblushing assurance could " re-solve " historical facts into the unsubstantial shadow of a dream. Now, myths do occur in connexion with many religions, and even in connexion with historical characters and astronomical facts. Yet it does not follow—

> That none of all our blood should know
> The shadow from the substance,

or that everything should be myth because myths exist.

Dealing with myth from the point of view of Astronomy, Mr. Maunder of the Greenwich Observatory urges [1] very forcibly that the myths which were devised to explain how the constellations came into being *could not have given rise to the idea of the existence of the constellations,* but must have sprung up long after men had shown a very considerable and fairly accurate knowledge of As-tronomy by arranging the stars and marshalling them into the form of constellations " upon a deliberate, and, in the strictest sense, a scientific plan. The science was real, if primitive." He goes on to say:—

The types of mind and states of civilization required for such a work as the construction of the constellations and for the incep-tion of myths are wholly diverse ; more than diverse, opposed and incompatible. All such myths, therefore, are not only later than the constellations but they imply that the constellations

---

[1] Annual Address, *Journal of Transactions of the Victoria Institute,* vol. xl., pp. 13–16.

had been known and their meaning forgotten or misunderstood. Such myths, therefore, are the evidence of knowledge on the down grade ; of astronomical knowledge lost ; not of astronomical knowledge incipent. The myths did not give rise to the constellations, but when the true knowledge of the constellations was forgotten, and the astronomical facts that they expressed were lost or misunderstood, then myths were invented to explain them ; they were the ditch into which the blind led the blind. And as with astronomical myths, so, no doubt, with other Nature-myths ; for myth is essentially the outcome of ignorance, the confusion of things that differ, the artificial attempt to explain that which is unintelligible to the narrator.

In astronomy, then, we find that the sequence—whether now or in primitive ages—is, observation, knowledge, then knowledge lost or misapprehended, then myth ; and not the converse (as it is usually contended), of myth, out of which observation grows, and thence knowledge is gained. . . . In the case of constellation-myths we have direct evidence that they are knowledge lost. An immense amount has been written upon myths in recent years, and the assumption has almost always been that they are primitive, original, the first stage towards knowledge. That is an assumption, and—in this case where we can test it—it is an untrue assumption.

If in science myth means the degradation of knowledge, does the very opposite of this hold good in religion ? Have we the right to assume that in religion myth is knowledge in the germ ?

If this scientist's conclusion be correct—and a very great deal can be said in its favour—then it appears that the knowledge of some of the very fundamentals of true religion—the existence of God, the After-Life, the value of prayer and sacrifice, the fact of sin, the need of a Saviour, the expectation of His coming in accordance with promise, etc.—existed in very early times among the ancestors of the human race, and that it was only later, when these great doctrines became half forgotten and misunderstood, that those myths arose to which the unthinking of our day are so fond of ascribing the origin of those doctrines of the Christian faith which inculcate these truths anew.

In this age of theories, which by their variety and mushroom-growth bear distinct witness to the danger of trying to draw final conclusions from the premises of our still extremely imperfect knowledge of the past, and to the folly of expecting our sand-castles to stand permanently in the face of the steadily advancing ocean of truth and certainty, we hear much of " Babylonian influence " on the Bible and on the Christian faith. Some even assure us that Christianity had its origin in Babylonian astronomical fables. There is a sufficient amount of verisimilitude in such a statement to make it dangerously misleading. We must enquire what degree of truth it contains and whether that truth in any way invalidates —and does not rather strengthen—the proofs of the Christian faith.

Although it is true that " between the polytheism of Babylonia and the monotheism of Israel a gulf is fixed which cannot be spanned," yet, as we have seen, certain resemblances are to be found between the language of the Hebrew Scriptures and that of the Babylonian tablets. But the contrast is far more striking. The " deep " (*tᵉhôm*) of Genesis i. 2 means the material though chaotic ocean, whereas the *Ti'âmat* of Babylonia, although the same word, denotes a fabulous female monster which fought with and was slain by Merodach. Then her body was used to form earth and sky. The " void " (*Bôhû*) of that passage is the word which in Babylonia became a goddess, Ba'u. To most unprejudiced people it would seem clear that the personification must be later than the plain, straightforward meaning of the words. At least in Latin people spoke of hope (*spes*) and harmony (*concordia*) before these qualities were worshipped as goddesses.

In some form, however, we may trace " Babylonian " myths, if not the earlier Babylonian science, over almost, if not quite, the whole world. The story of the slaughter of Ti'âmat by Merodach and the construction of heaven and earth out of her remains is reproduced, with the names changed, in China in the tale of P'ân Ku, in Persia [1] in Mânî's account of the giant Kunî, in India in the legend of Purusha, in Scandinavia in the fable of the fate of the giant Ymir. The " tree of life " in Babylonia came to be the Šumerian name for the vine (*Geš-ten*), but we find such a tree in the Pârijâta of Indra's paradise, in the Yggdrasill of Scandinavia, and the " Tree of the World " among the Bon-chos of Western Tibet, which has its roots in the Underworld and its highest branches in heaven, while in Greek mythology it bears the golden apples of the Hesperides.

Instance after instance of similar " borrowings," if such they can be called, will readily occur to the mind. The narrative of the Flood, found in different forms among almost every tribe and nation in the New World and in Oceania as well as in the Old World, is an instance of the tradition of an actual historical fact similarly preserved, handed down by tradition, or borrowed. How are such things to be accounted for ?

Dr. Alfred Jeremias holds that, from Babylonia, about 3,000 B.C., or a little earlier, a system of combined science and religion, founded upon " a purely astronomical

---

[1] It is said in the Fravardin Yasht that the " navel and surface of the Āryan lands " were made out of the body of Gayô-marethan (Kayomarth), the first man.

theory . . . spread over the whole world, and, exerting a different intellectual influence over every civilization, according to the peculiar character of each, it developed into many new forms . . . without any destructive effect on racial and national differences."

Is this theory of his easier to accept than the Biblical statement that Shinar (Šumer [1]) or Southern Babylonia was the cradle of the human race, and that after the Flood the earth was repeopled from that centre ? Hence the different families and tribes bore with them on their migration their common traditions, which in process of time became modified in details, though still very often agreeing with one another in essentials. As they carried away from their Babylonian home the narrative of the Flood and some crude cosmological allegories, is it unlikely that they took with them also whatever they had of religious rites and doctrines ? These are things which, as all history and experience show, though liable to corruption, perversion and misunderstanding, never really die out in a nation. Our own sacred wells, our fairy rings, the names of the days of the week, our Yule-tide festivities, our May-day dances, our superstitions, these and many other things are hoary survivals from a system or systems of religion otherwise well-nigh forgotten. There can be no doubt that, *in this sense*, Babylonian influence may be traced everywhere. But whether this fact is due to its having in some mysterious manner swept over the whole world as late as about 3,000 B.C., may well be questioned, until we have further evidence to prove it.

Christianity has never claimed to be an entirely new

[1] It is still disputed whether Šumer and Shinar are the same word. Shinar may denote the *whole* of Babylonia.

system of teaching, absolutely unconnected with everything which preceded it. It is a republication and completion of primeval revelation, a fulfilment of Divine promises (such as that in Gen. iii. 15). Hence it is very natural that we should discover in it, as we do, certain somewhat distant resemblances to matters mentioned in other forms in many earlier faiths. The Bible tells us of man's pristine belief in and communion with God, his fall into sin, God's acceptance of animal sacrifice, and the Divine promise of a coming Saviour. If this account is true—and in these matters the New Testament confirms the Old—an easier explanation presents itself than that of " borrowing " from Babylon about 3,000 B.C. Here again we trust that our ultra-credulous critics will pardon us for holding that " the old is better."

Comparative Religion is day by day throwing more and more light on some of these Biblical statements and confirming their strict and literal accuracy. To illustrate this let us select one of them and examine it—the statement that originally man worshipped the One True God, and Him alone.

If this be so, it follows that Monotheism historically preceded Polytheism, and that the latter is a corruption of the former. Let us briefly test this statement by referring to what is known of the most ancient religious ideas of some of the greatest nations belonging to different stocks—the Chinese, the Indian and Persian Âryans, the Babylonians, and the Egyptians.

The Chinese early recognized a power named T'ien (which also means the sky), which, like the Jehovah of the Old Testament, was pleased by good, and relentlessly punished evil.[1]

---

[1] Prof. Giles, at Oxford Congress for History of Religions : *Times* of September 18, 1908.

In the *Rig-Veda* there is a class of deities styled Asuras, who are vastly superior to the ordinary devas or "gods" that afterwards ousted them from their high position. The word *Asura* means "living," "active," [1] but is used only in reference to bodiless, spiritual life (*asu*), and is frequently connected in use with terms which imply wisdom. As a noun, *Asura* means Spirit, God. It is used in the *Rig-Veda* to denote a very lofty Being, and the word often occurs in very close connexion with Varuṇa, of whom we have already spoken. [2] Varuṇa himself seems to have at one time been regarded by the Indian Âryans as the one and only True God. Traces of belief in Monotheism occur even after the rise of Polytheism. Of this we quote a few passages in proof. In *Rig-Veda*, i. 164, śloka 46, we read : " They say ' Indra, Mitra, Varuṇa, Agni ' ; and then there is the divine fair-winged bird (*Garutmân*). In many ways do the sages speak of the One Being (*Ekam sat*) ; they say ' Agni, Yama, Mâtariśvan.' " In the *Atharva Veda* (x, 7, 13, 22, 27) it is said that all the thirty-three gods are the limbs or members (i.e., instruments) of Prajâpati, the " Lord of creatures." The ancient Sanskṛit Index to the *Veda*, in explanation of the former of these two passages, says : " There is just one deity, the Great Soul. He is called the Sun, for he is the soul of all beings. . . . Other deities are portions of him, and that is clearly stated by the Ṛishi, ' They say Indra,' " etc.

In Darius' Cuneiform Inscriptions at Mâl-i-Amîr and elsewhere, Ahura-Mazdâ (there called Auramazda) is spoken of as the Creator of Heaven and Earth, as the

---

[1] Grassmann, *Wörterbuch zum Rig-Veda.*
[2] P. 55.

Great God, and by other lofty titles. The language used of Him is such as might be employed by any Monotheist to-day. Only casual reference is made to " clan gods," who evidently occupied a very inferior place indeed in the King's estimation.

In the Gâthâs, ascribed to Zoroaster himself, Ahura-Mazdâ at times appears as the chief, almost the only, God, the other Amesha Speñtas seeming to rank rather as His attributes than as independent deities. But in later times, as other parts of the Avesta prove, Mithra, Anâ-hita and many other deities shared in the worship of the Zoroastrians, or *Mazdayasnians* (Mazdâ-worshippers) as they styled themselves. It is true that from the Avesta we learn that Zoroaster's work was that of a reformer, and that he opposed the polytheists or *daêva*-worshippers. This doubtless shows that before Zoroaster's time many or all of the Persians were polytheists ; but reformation consists not in the introduction of a new religion, but in recalling people to an earlier and purer form of faith.

Hence again we see that in Persia, as among the Indian Âryans, Monotheism preceded Polytheism.

Similarly we find that in later times in Arabia Muḥam-mad claimed to recall the people from the worship of very many inferior deities of the second rank to that of " God Most High," whose existence and unity they all theo-retically admitted, though letting Him be practically superseded by gods and goddesses of a far lower class.

In the code of Ḥammurabi (Amraphel), which contains laws of almost immemorial antiquity codified by that King, although many gods are mentioned by name in the Preface, dating from that King's time, yet in the Laws themselves language is used which is distinctly Mono-theistic. Oaths are to be taken " in the presence of

God " (*maḫar Ilim*), no name of the Deity being mentioned. For example, it is said : " If a visitation of God (*libit Ilim*) happen to a fold, or a lion kill, the shepherd shall declare himself innocent before God (*maḫar Ilim*), and the owner of the fold shall suffer the damage." [1] This shows clearly that " God " was originally recognized in Babylonia before He was forgotten in the gradual corruption of religion which finally filled the land with a multitude of idols.

Lastly, we turn to Egypt, where we have the *Precepts of Kaqemna* (in the time of the Fourth Dynasty) and those of *Ptaḥ-Ḥotep* (under the Fifth Dynasty)—works which were ancient classics in Moses' days—and in them we find the same phenomenon still more clearly. Of the " God " (*Neter*) there so constantly mentioned, Dr. Budge writes [2] : " The Being whose ways are inscrutable, who rules the world on a definite plan (*sekher*), who confers possessions on men, who demands obedience from man and expects him to bring up his children in the fear of him and to deal kindly with his neighbours, can surely be no other than God. If the writers of the Precepts referred in their minds to any of the gods of Egypt, they would have added their names. The Being referred to cannot be Osiris, for in no text are such attributes ascribed to him. We must, it seems to me, conclude that only God, the Creator of All, could be spoken of in this manner."

Elsewhere [3] he says : " The Egyptians believed in the existence of One Great God, self-produced, self-existent,

---

[1] Col. xxxviii., lines 76–81.
[2] *Osiris and the Egyptian Resurrection*, vol. i., pp. 350, 351.
[3] Op. cit., Preface.

almighty, and eternal, who created the 'gods,' the heavens and the sun, moon and stars in them, and the earth and everything on it, including man and beast, bird, fish, and reptile. They believed that He maintained in being everything which He had created, and that He was the support of the universe and the Lord of it all. Of this God they never attempted to make any figure, form, likeness or similitude, for they thought that no man could depict or describe Him, and that all His attributes were quite beyond man's comprehension. On the rare occasions on which He is mentioned in their writings, He is always called *NETER* " ⌐⌐ (the divine hieroglyph)], " i.e. ' God,' and besides this He has no name. No proof of any kind is forthcoming which shows that the Egyptians ever entirely forgot the existence of God, but they certainly seem to have believed that He had altogether ceased to interfere in human affairs, and was content to leave the destinies of man to the care of the ' gods ' and spirits."

These are a few facts out of many which might be adduced. It is impossible to explain them away. Taken together they serve to show that, as the Bible asserts, man at the very beginning of his history knew the One True God. This implies a Revelation of some sort, and traces of that Revelation are still to be found in many ancient faiths.

Christ came not to destroy but to fulfil. He came to complete the religious education of the human race, to reconcile man to God in Himself, to be the one Sacrifice for sin, of which all others were but types and shadows, to undo the Fall, and to annul death. Can it be said that He has failed ?

Christianity is related to other Faiths as their complement, their fulfilment, their realization. And when that which is perfect is come, then that which is in part should be done away.

INDEX

Printed by BUTLER & TANNER, *Frome and London.*

INTERESTING MISSIONARY LITERATURE.

ST. PAUL AND HIS CONVERTS : Studies in Typical New Testament Missions. By the REV. HARRINGTON C. LEES, M.A. Cloth, 1s. *net.*

"The writer is always fresh and instructive, his work is sound and of great value. Indeed, we have not often come across so much in so little as this book gives us, and we most heartily recommend it."—*Missionary Review.*

THE DUST OF DESIRE.
By EVELYN S. KARNEY (C.E.Z.M.S.). Introduction by the Rev. W. ST. CLAIR TISDALL, D.D. Cloth, 3s. 6d *net.*

The book is written in so interesting a fashion that many who know nothing of the Oriental faiths or sacred books will yet be able to follow the story and enjoy it.

BY THE SAME AUTHOR.

BROKEN SNARES. Preface by the BISHOP OF DURHAM. Cloth, 1s. 6d. *net.*

"A vivid picture of the everyday life of the worker abroad."—*Our Missions.*

WAITING ORDERS.
Preface by the Rev. GEORGE HANSON, D.D. Cloth, 1s. *net.*

"This is a delightful book, and should be widely circulated."—*Record.*

INDIAN IDYLLS.
By ANSTICE ABBOTT. Introduction by GEORGE SMITH, LL.D., C.I.E. With Eight Illustrations. Cloth, 3s. 6d. *net.*

"We cordially agree with Dr. George Smith that these stories of life among our Indian sisters have a distinct literary charm, and we trust their perusal may lead many who are contemptuous or indifferent to missionary work to reconsider their attitude. The illustrations are worthy of the letterpress."—*Record.*

MISSIONARY RECITATIONS FOR CHILDREN.
By FRANCES STRATTON. Cloth, 1s. 6d. *net.*

A volume of verse dealing with Foreign Missions, intended for recitation by boys and girls, either singly or in groups, at missionary meetings, Sunday-school entertainments, etc.

A VISIT TO CHINA'S MISSIONS.
By REV. F. S. WEBSTER, M.A. Preface by WALTER B. SLOAN. Fully Illustrated by Photographs specially obtained *en route.* Cloth, 2s. 6d. *net.*

"A magnificently illustrated and intensely interesting volume."—*Church Gazette.*

THE SPLENDOUR OF A GREAT HOPE.
By the VENERABLE ARTHUR EVANS MOULE, B.D. Foreword by His Grace the LORD ARCHBISHOP OF CANTERBURY. Cloth, 3s. 6d. *net.*

MISSIONS AND SOCIOLOGY. By the REV. T. E. SLATER (L.M.S.). 1s. *net.*

"All interested in the social aspect of Christianity in reference to mission work should read it."—*Aberdeen Journal.*

HANDY ATLAS TO CHURCH AND EMPIRE.
Edited by the BISHOP OF EDINBURGH and the late REV. C. BARTON, M.A. Comprising 120 Maps, Plates, and Statistical Tables, showing the Advance of Missions in all parts of the British Empire to the Present Day. Cloth, 1s. 6d. *net.*

MR. EUGENE STOCK : "It is simply delightful, full of valuable information."

INDIAN FOLK-TALES. Side-Lights on Village Life in the Central Provinces. By E. M. GORDON. Cheap Edition. Cloth, 1s. 6d. *net.*

"The observations here recorded are of immense value to all who are interested in Missions to India."—*Church Times.*

EASTERN PACIFIC LANDS. Tahiti and the Marquesas Islands.
By F. W. CHRISTIAN. With Fifty-seven Illustrations and Seven Maps. Cloth, 7s. 6d. *net.*

The work includes, amongst other things, many feelingly-drawn pen-pictures of the social condition of the natives, and lays great stress upon the urgent need of evangelization of the Marquesans by educated Polynesian teachers from the neighbouring native Churches of Hawaii and Rarotonga.

COVERLEIGH RECTORY. By MARY D'AGUILAR. Cloth, 3s. 6d.

"The needs of missionaries on the field are vividly portrayed."—*Methodist Times.*

LONDON : **ROBERT SCOTT,** PATERNOSTER ROW, E.C.

THEOLOGICAL AND DEVOTIONAL WORKS.

By the Rev. H. G. GREY, M.A.

A COMMENTARY ON ST. PAUL'S EPISTLE TO THE ROMANS. Cloth, 3s. 6d. net.

By the Rev. Principal H. G. GREY; being the first Volume in the Readers' Commentary. Other Volumes in preparation :—THE FIRST EPISTLE TO THE CORINTHIANS : by the Rev. DAWSON WALKER, D.D. THE SECOND EPISTLE TO THE CORINTHIANS : by the Rev. F. S. GUY WARMAN, B.D. THE EPISTLE TO THE GALATIANS : by the Rev. CYRIL EMMET, M.A. Further announcements will be made in due course ; full particulars may be obtained from the Publisher.

THE MINISTRY OF THE WORD AND SACRAMENTS.

By JOHN WILLIAM DIGGLE, D.D. (Bishop of Carlisle). Crown 8vo, Cloth Gilt, 2s. 6d. *net*.

INTRODUCTION TO DOGMATIC THEOLOGY ON THE BASIS OF THE XXXIX. ARTICLES of the Church of England.

By the late E. A. LITTON, M.A. New Edition, Revised by the Rev. H. G. GREY, M.A., of Wycliffe Hall, Oxford. Introductory Note by the Rev. Principal A. J. TAIT. Demy 8vo, Cloth, 10s. 6d. *net*.

TOWARDS A PERFECT MAN : Studies in the Making of Character (Second Series). By the Rev. HENRY W. CLARK. Cloth, 2s. *net*.

By the same Author.

STUDIES IN THE MAKING OF CHARACTER. Cloth, 2s. net.

LAWS OF THE INNER KINGDOM. Cloth, 3s. 6d. net.

"Full of seed-thought to preachers and teachers."—*The Churchman.*

SERMONS ON SOCIAL SUBJECTS.

Arranged and Edited by the Rev. PERCY DEARMER, M.A. Cloth, 2s. *net*.

Vital Questions of the Day by the following leading Theologians : J. G. ADDERLEY, M.A. ; Preb. J. WAKEFORD, B.D. ; J. E. WATTS-DITCHFIELD, M.A. ; A J. CARLYLE, D.D. ; Canon MASTERMAN, M.A. ; PERCY DEARMER, M.A. ; Canon SCOTT HOLLAND, D.D.

THE LIFE HEREAFTER. Thoughts on the Intermediate State. 2s. *net*.

By the Rev. EDWARD HICKS, D.D., D.C.L.

THE CROSS IN HOLY SCRIPTURE. A Study of the Nature and Significance of Christ's Redemptive Work. Cloth, 2s. *net*.

By the Rev. JAMES LITTLE, B.A., S.T.D.

LOMBARD STREET IN LENT.

Edited by the Rev. PERCY DEARMER, M.A. Introduction by the Rev. Canon SCOTT HOLLAND, D.D. Cloth, 1s. 6d. *net*.

GAINS AND LOSSES.

By the Right Rev. G. H. S. WALPOLE, D.D., Bishop of Edinburgh. Stiff Purple Wrapper, 1s. *net* ; Cloth Boards, 1s. 6d. *net*.

A SIMPLE GUIDE TO HOLY COMMUNION. Cloth, 6d.

By the Right Rev. G. H. S. WALPOLE, D.D., Bishop of Edinburgh.

IMITATION OF CHRIST.

By THOMAS A KEMPIS. Faithfully Rendered into English Rhythm after the manner in which it was written. Preface by the late Canon LIDDON. Cloth, 2s. *net* ; Velvet Leather, 4s. 6d. *net*.

LONDON : ROBERT SCOTT, PATERNOSTER ROW, E.C.

BOOKS FOR PREACHERS AND TEACHERS.

SERMONS IN A NUTSHELL. A New Handbook of Outlines for Busy Speakers. By J. ELLIS (*Editor of the " Tool Basket " Series*). Cloth, 1s. net ; Interleaved Edition, 1s. 6d. net.
A Treasury of Helpful Suggestions.

IN QUIETNESS AND CONFIDENCE. Fifty-six Readings for Sundays and Holy Days on various aspects of Christian experience. By the VEN. ARCHDEACON WYNNE, D.D. Cloth, 2s. 6d. net.

MINIATURE SERMONS FOR BUSY PEOPLE. By the REV. H. O. MACKEY. Cloth, 2s. 6d. net.

OUTLINE STUDIES. For Sermons and Addresses. By the REV. JAMES DINWOODIE. Cloth, 2s. 6d. net.

IDEALS FOR THE CHRISTIAN LIFE. By the REV. W. D. M. SUTHERLAND. Introduction by Rev. G. H. MORRISON. Cloth, 2s. 6d. net.
"A work of really original power."—*British Weekly.*

THE USE OF THE EYES IN PREACHING. Preaching and Speaking without Notes. By the REV. JOHN NEVILLE. Paper, 1s. net ; Cloth, 1s. 6d. net.

SUNDAY-SCHOOL TEACHING. Helps, Counsels, and Suggestions. By the REV. F. G. LLEWELLIN. Introductory Letter by the BISHOP OF LLANDAFF. Cloth, 1s. net.

TWO TREATISES ON THE CHURCH. By the REV. THOMAS JACKSON, D.D., and the REV. ROBERT SANDERSON, D.D. Preface by the LORD BISHOP OF DURHAM. Cloth, 3s. 6d. net.

THE MESSENGER OF GOD. Studies on Malachi. By DUGALD MACFADYEN, M.A. Cloth, 2s. net.

THE PROBLEM OF UNITY : A Symposium by Leaders of Evangelical Thought. Preface by the Right Hon. LORD KINNAIRD. Cloth, 1s. 6d. net.

TOOLS FOR TEACHERS. By WILLIAM MOODIE. Helpful for those engaged in the Moral and Religious Training of the Young. Cloth, 5s.

MY MATES. Sunday Talks to Young People. By J. J. BROWN. Cloth, 2s. net.

THE FULNESS OF THE GOSPEL. By D. L. MOODY. Cloth, 1s. 6d. net.

THE LORD'S TREASURES. Bible Talks with the Children. By MRS. HARDING KELLY. Cloth, 1s. 6d. net.

WORKS ON CONFIRMATION AND COMMUNION.

CONFIRMATION LECTURES. A Series of Notes on the Church Catechism. By the REV. CANON A. E. BARNES-LAWRENCE, M.A. Cloth, 1s. net.

CONFIRMATION. A Manual for Candidates and Teachers. By L. M. BAGGE. Preface by the Rev. Canon W. H. M. H. AITKEN. Cloth, 1s. 6d. net.

COMMUNION AND OFFERING. Simple Instructions upon the Office of Holy Communion. By the RIGHT REV. THE BISHOP OF EDINBURGH. Cloth, 1s. ; Leather, 2s. ; Lambskin, 3s. ; Persian Calf, 3s. 6d.

THE CHRIST IN HOLY COMMUNION. By the REV. T. A. GURNEY, M.A. Cloth, 1s. net.

Send for complete Catalogue, free by post.

LONDON: ROBERT SCOTT, PATERNOSTER ROW, E.C.

Primitive Man must have
been first a Monotheist and
to have drifted into Polytheism

175. Buddha's ethics
176 - Muslim - wine.
206 - Hospitals -

261.2
T61